Praise for *The Gen X Handbook for Middle Age*

"Finally, a book that gets Gen X—those of us who grew up with MTV, ashtrays in cars, Ronald Reagan and a front-row seat to the collapse of the Soviet Empire. *The Gen X Handbook for Middle Age* captures our grit, humor, and quiet rebellion."

—Rachel Campos-Duffy, FOX News host

"Lisa's book is about being a member of Gen X. She provides personal and universal insight into our changing world. It is a must read, funny, poignant, deeply honest and personal. When a writer lives through the eye of a hurricane, they can give witness to the towering, turbulent clouds of the eyewall, a wall of intense thunderstorms with the storm's strongest winds and heaviest rain, encircling the eye like a coliseum. So, buckle up Gen X and enjoy! No damage incurred except perception!"

—Robert Davi, actor, singer, iconic villain

"As a guy who's been through the muck, I can tell you Lisa De Pasquale's *The Gen X Handbook for Middle Age* nails it. This isn't some fluffy nostalgia trip; it's a raw, unfiltered look at a generation that learned to thrive in the chaos, not just survive it. Lisa gets the X vibe—tough, skeptical, and allergic to BS. If you're Gen X or just want to understand why we're the way we are and how we can get even better, this book's your field manual. Respect earned."

—Terry Schappert, former Army Special Forces, host of *Hollywood Weapons*

"In a world gone mad, Gen X has stayed sane. With practicality and humor, Lisa provides tips on leaning into that sanity. Recommend!"

—Jennifer Sey, founder and CEO of XX-XY Athletics and former senior VP and CMO at Levi Strauss & Co.

"I feel seen. I don't want to be a member of any club that will have me…except Gen X. Lisa perfectly illustrates exactly what the (truly) greatest generation needs right now, a bit of compassionate common sense."

—Ethan Suplee, actor and *American Glutton* podcast host

Also by Lisa De Pasquale

I Wish I Might
The Social Justice Warrior Handbook: A Practical Survival Guide for Snowflakes, Millenials, and Generation Z
Finding Mr. Righteous

The Gen X Handbook for Middle Age

The Gen X Handbook for Middle Age

The Pursuit of Health, Success, and Human Fulfillment

LISA DE PASQUALE

Post Hill
PRESS

A POST HILL PRESS BOOK
ISBN: 979-8-89565-122-3
ISBN (eBook): 979-8-89565-123-0

The Gen X Handbook for Middle Age:
The Pursuit of Health, Success, and Human Fulfillment

Cover design by Brett R. Smith and Eric Weathers

Post Hill Press
New York • Nashville
posthillpress.com

Published in the United States of America
1 2 3 4 5 6 7 8 9 10

TABLE OF CONTENTS

INTRODUCTION

In 2025, the first wave of Gen Xers turned sixty. Our band T-shirts are vintage or sold as reproductions at Walmart and Hot Topic. Our playground of old tires and hot metal are the basis of the multibillion-dollar CrossFit gym empire. Our toys are our highest value assets. Our movies are classics. Gen X—led by Elon Musk, Greg Gutfeld, Taylor Sheridan, and Joe Rogan—is at the top of media and pop culture. We are entering our Golden Age.

Boomer coworkers used to gather at the office with balloons that read "Over the Hill" and black napkins as they ate grocery store sheet cake with black icing. The theme was tombstones and death as they poked fun at the guy turning forty—FORTY. Now, discriminating (or making jokes) against people over forty is cause for a visit from human resources in most corporate offices. Ironically, Gen Xers are the only generation that can take a joke without making an HR complaint.

We are hitting our prime earning years in Trump's Golden Age. As a proud Gen Xer, I'm here to shepherd you through the best years of your life. My qualifications? My life got significantly better after forty: I lost 170 pounds, got plastic surgery to improve my life and fitness, became debt free, moved to another state to improve my finances, and found love. This book is packed with tips for making middle age your best years. For Gen X, the good ol' days are still to come.

You may be wondering if you're Generation X. You qualify if you can check off one of these items:

- Born between 1965 and 1980
- A member of the Brat Pack
- Born in the early 1980s and:
    - Served in the military
    - Had a job at sixteen or earlier
    - Enjoyed pop culture influenced by an older brother or sister

Health

HOW TO LOSE 170 POUNDS—THE EASY WAY!

On my fortieth birthday, there were no "Over the Hill" balloons and tombstone decorations. The parties may have been outdated, but it was beginning to look like a reality for me. I was 5'4" and over 300 pounds, more than $50,000 in credit card debt, unemployed, and single. I was in desperate need of a makeover montage. Unfortunately, three minutes of hair, makeup, and messy closet footage would not be enough for me.

The last time I was a normal weight was the day I was born—a few weeks early and under six pounds. As a young, chubby girl, I was often told I looked like Rudy's friend Peter on *The Cosby Show* and Chunk from *The Goonies*; it didn't help that I had the same boyish haircut as those two. There were a ton of fad diets in the 1980s and, even if they weren't for children, I was down to try them. I stole Dexatrim from a friend's medicine cabinet. I was entered into a clinical trial for some kind of nutritional "cookie" at Florida State University (the cookies were good if you slathered them in peanut butter!). Like so many adults around me, I also tried SlimFast, minus the sensible meals. By fifth grade, I was just over 150 pounds and mastered playing sick on school weigh-in days so I wouldn't have to do it in front of the class. Yes, Gen X was subject to getting weighed in front of the ENTIRE CLASS. No wonder we're so cynical.

By my senior year in high school, I found some success and finally got under 200 pounds with a "physician-supervised" program that emphasized sensible meals, protein bars, and weekly vitamin B12 shots to supposedly increase metabolism. I didn't lose enough to get asked out for prom, but I was gradually getting to "normal, with just some baby fat" territory.

Then came the independence of my college years. Meals were leftover bagels before they were thrown away from my college job at Starbucks and anything from the ninety-nine cents menu at the Wendy's near my other job at Gap Outlet. As I progressed in my career at Gap (lead cashier!), I made enough to write checks that I knew wouldn't be cashed for several days to pay for a meal at a local restaurant while studying.

After graduating from college, I moved to the Washington, DC area and worked in conservative politics. I lived the suburb life, which included grocery store runs where I could finally buy whatever I wanted, because not only did I have a full-time, low-paying job and no supervision, but I also had credit cards. As I wrote more and made a couple of TV appearances, I was introduced to adult bullying via hate mail. It was pre-Healthy At Every Size Left, so the gates were wide open for those who disagreed with me to call me fat. Of course, post-Healthy At Every Size Left didn't change that.

As my notoriety in the movement grew, so did the number on the scale. By the time I shared the stage with Rush Limbaugh at Conservative Political Action Conference 2009, I was 320 pounds.

We both wore all black—it was very slimming! The emails and comments I got about my appearance were bad, but still paled in comparison to what I thought about myself. Around that time Rush began talking about his weight loss on his radio show. In May 2009, I decided to follow suit and got lap-band surgery. Instead of loosening your belt after a big meal, it's the equivalent of wearing an extra tight belt before every meal, except the belt was on my esophagus. It was like eating like a dainty Victorian lady with small nibbles and lots of chewing.

I lost seventy pounds!

Then I slowly gained it back. Like my childhood hack of spreading peanut butter on the weight loss cookies to make them taste good, I gravitated toward foods that were easier to eat despite the restrictions from the lap-band.

In October 2018, I was officially a failed weight loss surgery patient when I was back over 300 pounds. I went to another bariatric surgeon about adjusting the lap-band. I was told that they no longer did that surgery or maintenance for it, as time had shown weight loss was less likely to last with that surgery. The surgeon told me that gastric bypass has continued to be the gold standard. Like the lap-band surgery and all fad diets, gastric bypass had its share of failures and successes. There were also the usual complications for any surgery and added risks of one that reroutes your digestive system. However, I needed to know—and for my friends and family to know—that I had at least tried the most drastic option short of wiring my jaw shut. If I ended up being a death by morbid obesity statistic, they would have comfort in knowing I tried it all.

The hardest part of the decision wasn't the possible complications or losing food as a coping mechanism, but that I could do it and still fail. A week before the surgery, I went to my first Bible study gathering and a verse from the speaker hit me—"I have set before you life and death, blessing and cursing. Therefore, choose life." (Deuteronomy 30:19)

My decision was easy: I wasn't choosing another way to lose weight or save face after dying, I was choosing life.

The most common comment about weight loss surgery is that it's taking the easy way out. I already knew from my first experience that wasn't always true. Food choice would continue to be an issue for me. Now in my late forties, I also needed to add more movement. Several months after recovering from weight loss surgery, I began a daily yoga practice by following videos I saved from YouTube. The videos were generally ten to twenty-five minutes and for "plus-size bodies." They were low impact but the point wasn't to burn calories. I needed to build a habit. I found myself skipping errands on the way home from work because I was getting antsy from missing this habit. As I lost weight, I started adding harder yoga classes that were made for all bodies. Yoga with Adriene's YouTube channel was a new habit and obsession.

By early 2021, I had lost over 130 pounds. Another plateau was on the horizon and it was time to add a new challenge. As I continued to age, building muscle was also important for keeping up with a slowing metabolism. I went back to YouTube and searched for videos on weightlifting. I began working them into my yoga schedule. I was proud of myself for staving off the COVID 15 (or 20 or 30 pounds of weight gain) as I transitioned from working in an office to working at home full-time. Like my college and early career years, working at home meant I could eat whatever I wanted alone and without judgment. To avoid those obstacles to my goal, I continued to log my food and weight every day to stay accountable. Working from home was also an opportunity to use my laziness as a workout tool. I removed the friction of a daily commute and then having to change into workout clothes when I got home. Instead, I started the day in my workout clothes and turned my office into my workout room. The yoga mat and weights stayed out 24-7.

It was just enough to keep me on a steady one to three pound loss per month.

Then I fell in love and moved to Texas.

I enjoyed cooking and baking for him (okay, us) and put on about twenty-five pounds in a year. It was time to add another tool to my toolbox.

I found the perfect training relationship for me—Elissa, a certified personal trainer who used to be my boss. In my mind, not showing up for a workout or not doing my best while lifting was akin to not showing up for work. I was an overachiever in my career and approaching workouts with this mindset worked for me. Working with Elissa for several months, along with cutting back on my baking and portions, helped me get to a weight of 150 pounds. In total, I had lost 170 pounds. I didn't achieve the cliché of getting to my high school weight—I got to my elementary school weight!

Workout gurus will tell you to "find your hard" by pushing yourself to the limit and challenging yourself in every workout. That doesn't have to be step one, though: instead, embrace your inner slacker and find your easy.

Meal plan to take away the decision-making that could derail you. Always have a couple quick, easy meals frozen or with fresh ingredients on hand that you enjoy that will be faster than UberEats.

Find an activity that makes daily movement an easy task. As a Gen Xer, you'll soon use the boredom during an easy workout to *want* to move on to the next challenge.

Make it fun. If you love nostalgia like me, you'll love writing your goals and workouts in your Trapper Keeper. Make a music playlist list that makes you want to move. Buy workout clothes that give you main character energy from *Perfect*, *Flashdance*, or *Rocky*.

Be a weight loss punk. It's totally punk rock to ignore the haters. No matter what combination of weight loss tools you use—carnivore, weight loss surgery, semaglutide, CrossFit, intermittent fasting—there will always be haters who say another way is better because it is harder or faster or natural. You know what motivates you; do what is motivating, successful, and easy for you to maintain.

But also remember, we're Gen X. There is a time for fun and easy and a time to just do it anyway. As Greg Gutfeld noted in a video for PragerU, "Fitness is one bank where you deposit effort and you build a portfolio of reward."

Working out isn't like Social Security: you'll actually see the benefits one day!

There is no finish line but there are moments to celebrate, moments when you could have done better and moments when you did the best you could. Actor and *American Glutton* podcast host Ethan Suplee said, "The finish line is death. There is no 'after'—this is a life-long process."

You don't want to sprint to the finish line. This mindset makes it easier to know my body will always be a work in progress. When I say my secret is to do everything all the time, I'm not being facetious. Life is about choices—some easy and some hard. I chose life—the "easy" choice.

HOW TO TOPPLE THE GENERATIONAL FOOD PYRAMIDS

The ultimate healthy boomer breakfast was a bran muffin; for a fruit option, there was a blueberry muffin! There were also various cereals like Grape-Nuts and Total. There definitely wasn't room for their parents' bacon and eggs unless you had a death wish. Boomers settled on eggs as the devil's snack when the American Heart Association warned in the 1960s that people shouldn't consume more than three eggs per week. Like social distancing six feet from others during COVID and eight eight-ounce glasses of water per day, the recommendation didn't appear to be based on science, but on being a simple number Americans could remember.

Thanks, but I'll stick to getting my 8,675,309 steps per year as my guiding fitness principle.

In the U.S., the food pyramid has long been a symbol of dietary guidance, but its iterations over the years have often been met with skepticism. Let's explore the cultural and dietary shifts through three generational food pyramids, each reflecting the eating habits and food trends of their eras.

The Boomer Food Pyramid

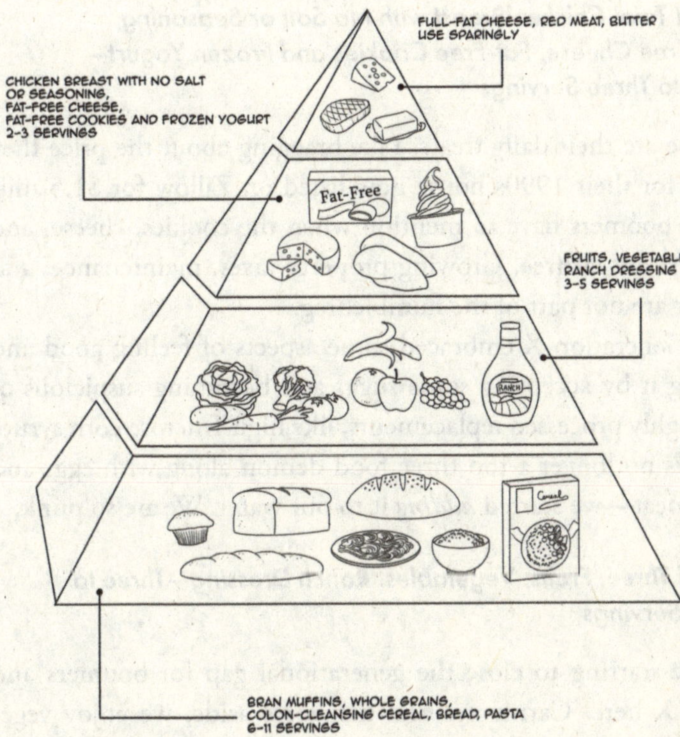

Level One: Full-Fat Cheese, Red Meat, Butter—Use Sparingly

Something had to give with the "if it feels good, do it" generation, and it was nutrient-rich red meat and eggs. They also loved replacing red meat with turkey—turkey bacon, turkey sausage, turkey meatloaf. They were the Bubba Gumps of turkey cuisine.

Generation X, however, embraced meat and the carnivore diet. As John Bender said, "Being bad feels pretty good, huh?"

Level Two: Chicken Breast with No Salt or Seasoning, Fat-Free Cheese, Fat-Free Cookies and Frozen Yogurt—Two to Three Servings

These are their daily treats. Like bragging about the price they paid for their 1990s house now listed on Zillow for $1.5 million, boomers have to mention when the cookies, cheese, and yogurt are fat-free. Growing property taxes, maintenance, and sugar are not part of the humblebrag.

Generation X embraced some aspects of feeling good and doing it by accepting some sugar and becoming suspicious of its highly processed replacements, like high-fructose corn syrup. Salt is no longer a top three food demon along with eggs and red meat—we started *adding* it to our water. We are so punk.

Level Three: Fruits, Vegetables, Ranch Dressing—Three to Five Servings

We're starting to close the generational gap for boomers and Gen X here. Carnivores and ketovores aside, we enjoy vegetables. But now we're in charge: we ditched the slimy brussel sprouts, so we'll take them roasted or fried. We'll still share the ranch or—better yet—a rich, lemony aioli.

Level Four: Bran Muffins, Whole Grains, Colon-Cleansing Cereal, Bread, Pasta—Six to Eleven Servings

Bran flakes have been available since 1915 and Raisin Bran in 1942. After living through the Golden Age of cereals—Trix, Fruit Loops, Apple Jacks, Lucky Charms, Cap'n Crunch—all invented in the 1950s, they needed a cleanse.

The 1970s and 1980s was the heyday for bran. It was having its moment as part of a complete breakfast for the busy boomer. By lunch, they were easing into more carbs with feel-good "whole wheat" bread. For dinner, rice, beans, and pasta meals opened a new world of safe and familiar ethnic food to get dinner on the table in a flash. Single moms were working and, in addition to feeling like chicken tonight and shaking and baking, there was an array of Hamburger or Tuna Helper in the pantry. Boxed dinners were also simple enough that latchkey kids could cook for themselves.

The Millennial Food Pyramid

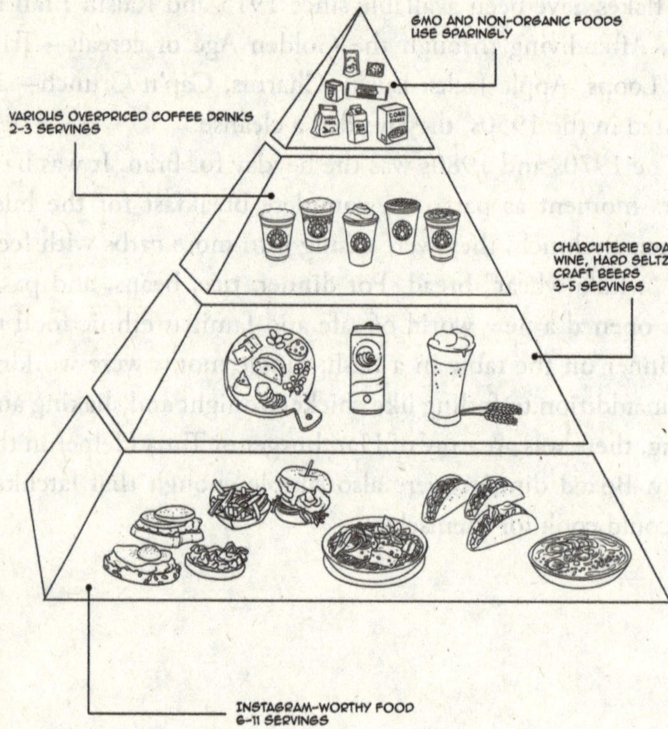

Level One: Genetically Modified Organism and Nonorganic Foods—Use Sparingly

While Generation X was at ground zero in doubting Big Food's pyramid, our millennial colleagues and kids really continued the battle. Like luxury logos, they seek out the organic and non-GMO labels. It's a virtue signal of their values and what they can afford.

Level Two: Various Overpriced Coffee Drinks—Two to Three Servings

Gen Xers link coffee to work and responsibility; caffeine is a tool to get through the morning. Millennials view coffee drinks as self-care. It became a movement, but not the functional kind. For millennials, it was about treating themselves to dessert any time of day—a major win for marketing executives.

Level Three: Charcuterie Boards, Wine, Hard Seltzers, Craft Beers—Three to Five Servings

Millennials love to entertain. Nothing shows sophistication and adulting like a nicely composed charcuterie board; all they did was upgrade their Lunchables. They came of drinking age at the same time as small-batch beers, American boutique wineries, and hard seltzers.

Level Four: Instagram-Worthy Food—Six to Eleven Servings

Camera phones leveled up food consumption. Like organic labels, what millennials eat signals their open-mindedness and station in life. As they get older, they straddle the line of wanting to be in on the trends (avocado toast and acai bowls) and the dive you haven't heard of with authentic pho.

The Generation Z and Generation Alpha Pyramid

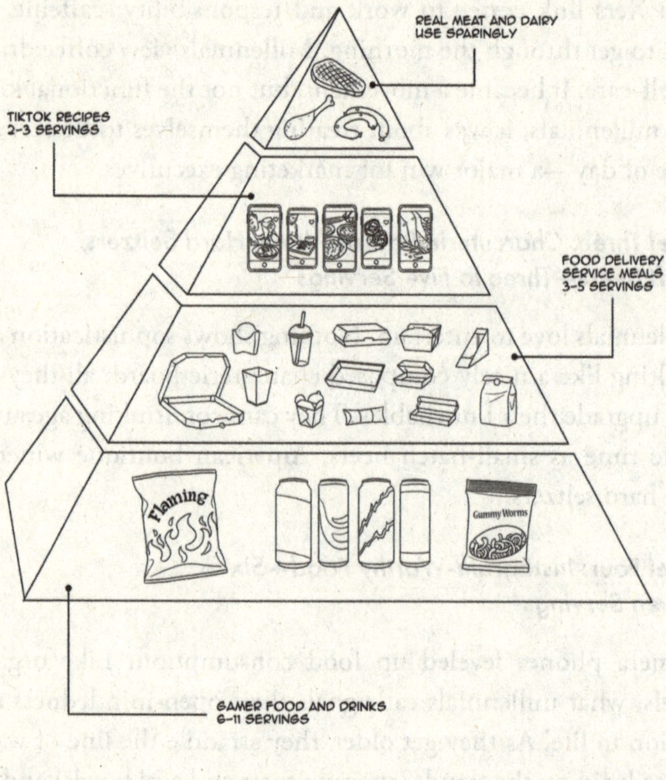

Level One: Real Meat, Dairy, and Peanuts—Use Sparingly

The Gen X and millennial generations dabbled in veggie burgers, but Gen Z and Gen Alpha went whole lab-created hog into plant-based meats and milks, to the point that meat and milk no longer have a meaning until a company gets sued for using the words. Due to the growing prevalence of allergies, peanuts are a universal no-no food in public spaces.

Level Two: TikTok Recipes—Two to Three Servings

The term "recipe" is used loosely. There are water recipes of elaborate concoctions of flavorings that question the definition of water—Gen Xers knew it as Kool-Aid. There are TikTok hacks for making a cream sauce from a block of cream cheese, water, and dried pasta that makes one question the definition of "hack." There is a positive aspect of trying these TikTok recipes, though—it prepares them for trying new things and for failure when a recipe doesn't come out right.

Level Three: Food Delivery Service Meals—Three to Five Servings

Postmates, Uber Eats, Grubhub, and DoorDash are staples at mealtime. Following their surge during the COVID era, accounts linked to their parents' bank accounts became as common as sharing a cell phone plan.

Level Four: Gamer Food and Drinks—Six to Eleven Servings

Living next to a park has taught me one thing about Gen Z and Gen Alpha—they're all inside. I mostly see neighborhood kids on Halloween, and every year, I recognize fewer and fewer costumes because they're dressed as video game characters. Their snacks are manufactured for their attention span—quick hits of spicy, sour, or sweet while on pause.

So, where does this leave Gen X? We're not immune to the powers of Big Food. When McDonald's brought back Happy Meals in retro plastic Halloween buckets in 2022 and collector cups in 2023, it wasn't for our kids and grandkids—they were for us and our love for nostalgia. Ask me how many Happy Meals I got with a cheeseburger without a bun and apples instead of fries (three). Ask me how many Quarter Pounder with Cheese (and again, with no bun) meals with Collector's Cups I got (six). Countering our nostalgia, however, is our distrust of Big Food and the government telling us what to eat.

Prior to making America healthy again, the proposed 2025–2030 US Dietary Guidelines continued the government's willful incompetence in guiding the public with the prioritization of plant-based proteins, dairy recommendations, and the lack of guidance on ultra-processed foods (UPFs). The Dietary Guidelines Advisory Committee's updated, 421-page tome no one will read, prioritized plant-based proteins like beans and legumes over red meat. They argue plant-based diets are healthier and more sustainable, while critics of the guidelines stress the nutritional value and bioavailability of animal proteins, particularly for vulnerable populations like older adults (that's us now). In other words, the bureaucrats put political philosophies above health.

The guidelines' omission of strong recommendations against UPFs (despite their links to obesity and chronic diseases) is problematic, to borrow a millennial and Gen Z phrase. Is it to avoid an explanation of why highly processed, plant-based "meats" are healthier than a good steak? Some nutritionists argue for stronger evidence to guide policies while insisting caution in promoting healthier alternative food philosophies like carnivore, keto, and paleo that used to just be known as food. The inclusion of dairy remains contentious, with some advocating for plant-based substitutes and "equity" for lactose-intolerant populations, while others defend its nutritional value.

Concerns about industry influence on the guidelines persist, with critics of old dietary guidelines urging the government to prioritize unbiased science. However, if COVID taught us anything, it might be that you also can't trust the science.

Like the Frankenfood, a lot of processing is required to get a cashew to taste as good as a sharp, aged cheddar. Gen Xers grew up with a healthy dose of disappointment; sometimes you didn't win the trophy. Sometimes you missed your favorite show and waited months until the rerun. Sometimes they ran out of the toy before you got it, enduring the agony of watching less-deserving kids play with it. And sometimes, your gut tells you that you can no longer eat cheese or nightshades. As we were told growing up, life isn't fair.

Thankfully, Gen X has never really trusted the government and we are now in the Golden Age of health and fitness. Political food philosophies will come and go, including raw foodism, flexitarianism, or veganism. To quote Ferris Bueller, "Not that I condone fascism, or any -ism for that matter. -Isms in my opinion are not good. A person should not believe in an -ism, he should believe in himself. I quote John Lennon, 'I don't believe in Beatles, I just believe in me.'"

Don't trust the man in white lab coat selling you neon-colored cereal and Frankenfood. Being a punk means eating red meat, avoiding seed oils, and limiting UPFs. Don't trust the weird science, but do trust your body's response.

WORKING OUT AS SELF-CARE

An Australian study from the Griffith University School of Medicine and Dentistry suggested that increasing exercise after forty could extend life expectancy by up to five years, or even eleven years, for those who are currently the least active. Analyzing US data, researchers found that matching the top 25 percent fitness level yields significant longevity benefits. The top 25 percent did about two hours and forty minutes of daily physical activity in total. Newsmax reported, "The researchers calculated that if everyone over 40 suddenly matched this activity level, it would raise everyone's expected life span by five years—from the 78.6 years it's now estimated to be to nearly 84 years."

The Center for Community Solutions, an Ohio-based group focused on public health and policy, highlighted the growth of stress experienced or perceived by people in the United States. Harris Poll survey data point to crime, inflation, political unrest, and racial tension as major concerns. The Center claimed that discrimination and systemic racism exacerbate stress for non-white individuals, often resulting in burnout for activists and policy advocates. Of course, this isn't the activist experience, but the human experience.

The Center said "self-care" was originally a medical concept for managing physical ailments. It evolved during the Civil Rights Movement and women's rights movement into a political act. For example, the Black Panther Party hosted community events that offered free clinics and healthy food as resistance against governmental neglect and police harassment. On the Center's website, Natasha Takyi-Micah wrote, "Some women leaders from the Civil Rights era were engaged in self-care. Ericka Huggins and Angela Davis of the Black Panther Party used yoga, mindfulness, and meditation practices while incarcerated as a form of self-care. Rosa Parks practiced yoga for many years. Self-care wasn't viewed as a luxury, but as a technique for self-empowerment to continue to fight social injustices."

While our politics may clash, emphasizing self-care as health, rather than a luxury dependent on your bank balance, is empowerment we can agree on. When it comes to working out, exercise, and movement in general, it's also useful to think of it as mental self-care, not just a tool for weight loss or building muscle. There is more evidence every day suggesting exercise and a diet without UPFs reduce risk of dementia. The great news for Gen Xers is that it doesn't necessarily need to be another daily task for the to-do list. A sixteen-year study from Mexico City tracked 10,033 adults and found that weekend exercise, once or twice weekly, reduces mild dementia risk by 25 percent compared to inactivity, slightly outperforming regular workouts done three times a week. The research, published in the *British Journal of Sports Medicine*, showed that even limited exercise protects brain health and could substantially reduce dementia.

As we see our parents, heroes, and pop culture influences age, working out for mental health becomes more appealing and necessary. Gen Xers can add our own spin to self-care by viewing exercise as an integral part of the self-care trend. Want to treat yo self *and* workout? Even better! Buy a new workout set and light your most expensive candle.

THE MODERN MIXTAPE: BUILDING THE PERFECT WORKOUT PLAYLIST FOR DILFS AND MILFS

Whether recorded from the radio or from your dual cassette tape player, nothing beats the perfect mixtape. We may grumble about the superiority of physical media over digital, but making the perfect playlist has never been easier. No longer do you have to press play and record at the exactly the right second for a good transition. If you're having trouble on where to start, let these inspire you. Go to LisaDePasquale.com for the Spotify links to these playlists.

DILF Mix (Sixty Minutes)

What you enjoy listening to will largely depend on your hairstyle in the 1980s—mullet, feathered, hi-top fade, Jheri curl, shaved, new wave, and so on. Here's a playlist for the guys who had the best cars and the best faded band T-shirts.

"Eye of the Tiger" by Survivor (mandatory)
"Metal Health" by Quiet Riot
"Cult of Personality" by Living Colour
"Who Made Who" by AC/DC
"Crazy Train" by Ozzy Osbourne
"The Trooper" by Iron Maiden
"Welcome to the Jungle" by Guns N' Roses
"Dr. Feelgood" by Mötley Crüe
"Seek & Destroy" by Metallica
"Unchained" by Van Halen
"Painkiller" by Judas Priest
"Training Montage" by Vince DiCola
"Heart's on Fire" by John Cafferty
"Tush" by ZZ Top
"Dream On" by Aerosmith
"Only the Young" by Journey (cooldown/stretch)

MILF Mix (Sixty Minutes)

A mix of songs you might have listened to with the top down but that you now hear in a strip club.

"Physical" by Olivia Newton John (mandatory)
"Into the Groove" by Madonna
"Tainted Love" by Soft Cell
"Wake Me Up Before You Go-Go" by Wham!
"Flashdance...What a Feeling" by Irene Cara
"We Got the Beat" by the Go-Go's
"Relax" by Frankie Goes to Hollywood
"Pour Some Sugar on Me" by Def Leppard
"Cherry Pie" by Warrant
"Sweet Emotion" by Aerosmith

"Push It" by Salt-N-Pepa
"Walking On Sunshine" by Katrina and the Waves
"Take My Breath Away" by Berlin (cooldown/stretch)

My Personal Weightlifting Motivation Playlist from Spotify (Sixty Minutes)

"Black Betty" by Ram Jam
"Hair of the Dog" by Nazareth
"More Human Than Human" by White Zombie
"Mony Mony" by Billy Idol
"Bawitdaba" by Kid Rock
"Dragula" by Rob Zombie
"Twilight Zone" by Golden Earring
"Pour Some Sugar on Me" by Def Leppard
"Panama" by Van Halen
"Renegade" by Styx
"Push It" by Salt-N-Pepa
"Eye in the Sky" by the Alan Parsons Project (cooldown/stretch)

The Filthy Fifteen, Compiled by Tipper Gore and the Parents Music Resource Center (Sixty Minutes)

"Darling Nikki" by Prince
"Sugar Walls" by Sheena Easton
"Eat Me Alive" by Judas Priest
"Strap On 'Robbie Baby'" by Vanity
"Bastard" by Mötley Crüe
"Let Me Put My Love into You" by AC/DC
"We're Not Gonna Take It" by Twisted Sister

"Dress You Up" by Madonna
"Animal (F**k Like a Beast)" by W.A.S.P.
"High 'n' Dry (Saturday Night)" by Def Leppard
"Into the Coven" by Mercyful Fate
"Trashed" by Black Sabbath
"In My House" by Mary Jane Girls
"Possessed" by Venom
"She Bop" by Cyndi Lauper

YOUR MOVIE MONTAGE TRAINING WORKOUT

For this workout, you are the star of your movie training montage. Everyone is rooting for you. Put on your favorite motivational workout playlist because that's a key piece of your montage. This fifteen-minute routine will boost your energy and increase your chances of winning the big match or new client. It is most effective outside at dawn or at magic hour in the evening, but if that doesn't fit your schedule, do this whenever you are able.

Warm-Up

- Take five deep breaths. Inhale through nose for a count of four. Exhale from mouth for a count of eight. Picture your enemies and their advantages as you prepare for your workout.
- Thirty seconds of cat cow stretch.
- Roll wrists and ankle clockwise, then counterclockwise, eight times on each side.

- Arm circles clockwise, then counterclockwise, eight times on each side.
- Ten mountain climbers.

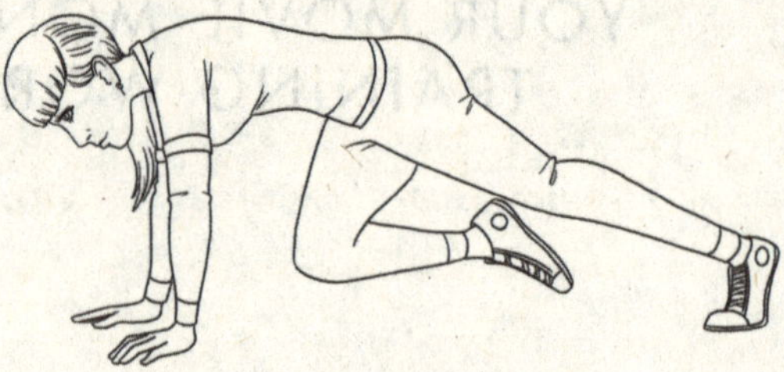

Round One

- Ten squats and presses with medium to heavy dumbbells.

- Ten push-ups—one-handed with a clap, on knees with a clap, or against a wall with a clap.

- Ten overhead medicine ball slams—squat to pick up a fifteen-pound medicine ball, lift overhead, slam on to the ground. If you don't have a medicine ball, this move can also be done with an axe while chopping wood.

- Thirty second break.

Round Two

- Ten reverse flies with the heaviest dumbbells you can manage to do a full set.

- Ten squat punches—use light dumbbells, if you can.

- Thirty second break.

Hearts and Abs on Fire Cardio Finish

- Standing scissor kick for thirty seconds.

- Sit-ups with four air punches at the top for thirty seconds.

- Repeat one to two times with no break in-between.

Cooldown

- Stretch various muscles like your high school crush is secretly watching and seeing you in a new light.

Celebrate

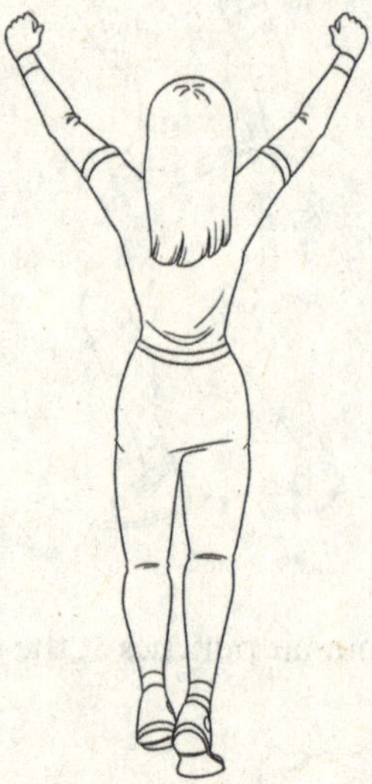

BIOHACK OR TURN OF THE CENTURY SCAM?

Remember when tabloids were splashed with photos of Michael Jackson in a hyperbaric oxygen chamber after getting severely burned during a Pepsi commercial? It looked like a see-through coffin and it was supposed to be another example of his eccentricity. Now when I Google "hyperbaric oxygen," I'm suggested the phrase "hyperbaric oxygen chamber near me." Nearly a dozen wellness centers deep in the heart of Texas offer this and other biohacking treatments for a variety of ailments and preventative measures. The promise of energy, restoration, and rejuvenation is intriguing. It's not just for Hollywood weirdos anymore.

Enjoy this fun quiz to identify if what you're doing is a popular biohacking trick (A), or from a traveling salesman in the late 1800s and early 1900s (B).

1. Get sunlight or artificial sunlight within the first twenty minutes of waking up to reset your circadian rhythm. This boosts your energy and cognitive function.

2. Use a mixture of mineral oil, beef fat, turpentine, and pepper to help alleviate symptoms of arthritis and sore muscles.
3. A blend of berberine, turmeric, black pepper, and milk thistle act as a natural semaglutide to regulate blood sugar.
4. To boost your body's natural immunity response, immerse yourself in a tub filled with ice water.
5. Massaging honey and beef tallow on your testicles helps moisturize and boost testosterone.
6. Distilled water and radium can improve impotence.
7. Photobiomodulation, also known as low-level laser therapy, stimulates collagen production and aids in muscle recovery.
8. Plug in your grounding sheets to help connect with the Earth's energy for a more restful night's sleep.
9. A vegetable compound, mixed with herbs and alcohol, helps with menstrual pain and menopause.
10. Reduce abdominal fat with electric vibrations of various frequencies applied directly to the target areas.

How did you do? An easy hack for identifying which is which is the switch from "fixing" an ailment to being preventative. Even though we're skeptical by nature, we're embracing some aspects of biohacking. If it doesn't work? Whatever.

Answers

1. A
2. B
3. A
4. A
5. A
6. B
7. A
8. A
9. B
10. B

YOUR PLASTIC SURGERY BUG-OUT BAG

Unlike our boomer predecessors and millennial successors, we are not focused on extreme transformations, but seek subtle, natural enhancements. We prioritize quality skin treatments to maintain a youthful appearance without heavy makeup because those baby oil and Hawaiian Tropic days are catching up with us. We are dealing with sun damage through laser treatments and skin routines. For more extensive changes, we are increasingly opting for surgeries like eyelid lifts and rhinoplasty when we can afford it later in life.

Menopause is also influencing many women from our generation to pursue facelifts for volume loss and skin elasticity. Dr. Sarmela Sunder, a Beverly Hills-based facial certified plastic surgeon told Allure magazine in 2024 that Gen X is "'[...]much more likely to do a facelift than to continue on with fillers at this point.'" Dr. Patrick Byrne, president of the American Academy of Facial Plastic and Reconstructive Surgery, added, "They feel that facelifting will give a more natural appearance." He said, "a lot of patients are skittish about filler because they've seen so many overinflated faces."

Thanks, *Real Housewives* franchise!

Gen X men tend to focus on preserving their looks with Botox and hair restoration. They grew up on HairClub for Men commercials and are ready to be customers. They also tend to wait longer than women to get any surgical procedures. In general, all of us want to look like better (and not just younger) versions of ourselves.

According to a 2022 study from the American Society of Plastic Surgeons, Gen X accounted for 35 percent of cosmetic surgeries, 46 percent of minimally invasive procedures, and 57 percent of Botox injections. Strategic combination treatments, like pairing facelifts with fillers or laser resurfacing, address multiple signs of aging while maintaining natural results. Despite their hesitancy, Gen X will make their procedure choice based on prevention to delay extensive procedures and stay ahead of aging.

I have not delved into the world of fillers (yet), but I do have lots of experience with plastic surgery. I consider my plastic surgeon to be my primary care doctor. I have no shame in talking about plastic surgery because it represents the hard work I've done: losing a massive amount of weight and saving the money to pay for it because I refused to finance it. I've had a brachioplasty (arm lift), thighplasty (thigh lift), mastopexy (breast lift), and abdominoplasty (360 degree body lift with a Fleur-de-Lis tummy tuck).

If you're preparing for the apocalypse of aging by getting plastic surgery that involves an overnight stay, here are my suggestions for what to pack in your plastic surgery bug-out bag:

- Phone charger and/or battery bank.

- Face wipes to give you the illusion of being clean.
- Extra underwear.
- Robe (hospital gowns have not changed in one hundred years).
- Comfortable outfit that minimizes any movement, like putting your arms over your head.
- Slip-on shoes and cozy socks.
- Nothing that will make you feel guilty for not using it, like a book. You're there to sleep and have your vitals monitored.
- Sleep mask and earplugs. If you're sensitive to light and noise, these are a must.
- Any medications you normally take. Bring extra in case your stay is extended.
- A comfort of home, such as a cashmere wrap or small lap blanket.

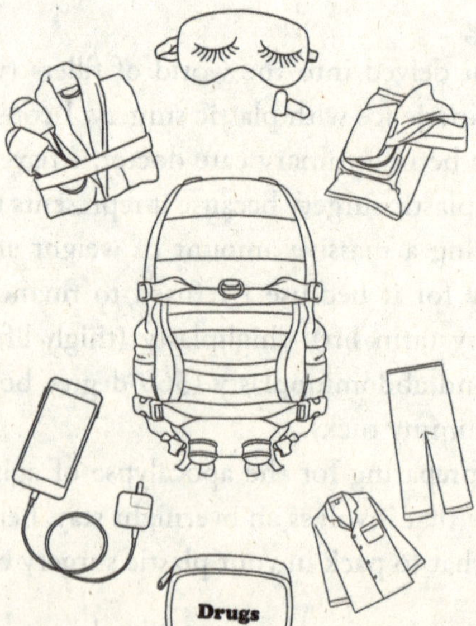

For after care, follow all the surgeon's instructions religiously and take advantage of follow-up appointments.

Gen X approaches plastic surgery with a unique, pragmatic mindset. In other words, "strike first, strike hard, no mercy."

GEN X MEDITATIONS AND MANTRAS: EMBRACING THE WHATEVER MINDSET

A 1980 study in the journal *Science* showed differences in pain perception between Nepalese porters and Western tourists, with the porters reporting less pain despite similar neurological responses. The study attributed the difference to the porters' Buddhist mindfulness practices, which involve focused, nonjudgmental awareness of the present moment. I call it the "Whatever Mindset."

Back pain? Whatever. Lost that big client? Whatever. Your 401(k) took a hit post-COVID? Whatever.

Additional research suggests mindfulness meditation lowers pain intensity by "uncoupling" the brain's pain-processing areas from those related to the sense of self. MRI scans reveal that mindfulness weakens connections between these regions, creating a mental distance from pain.

Experts recommend simple mindfulness practices, such as focusing on breathing or tying mindfulness to daily tasks, for sustained benefits. Even brief training can rewire the brain and improve pain perception. By letting go of attachment to pain, mindfulness enables a calmer, more stable state of mind, promoting healing and resilience.

Meditation can also be a cost-effective way to reduce stress. It can be practiced anywhere and incorporates various techniques, such as guided imagery, positive mantras, yoga, and deep breathing. For me, meditation helps me clear mental clutter, relax, and get in a quick nap (if a guided meditation is more than thirty minutes and the yogi has a soothing voice).

There are several apps like Calm and Headspace but my favorite way to find meditation prompts is YouTube. Some of my favorite channels are Christian-based (Exhale Fear and Alabaster Co). I also search for goals I have for a session, such as productivity or relaxation, and pick the one with the speaker with the best voice.

Don't be hesitant to try it, Gen Xers. Here are some mantras to ease into a meditation practice. These are most effective in a quiet space that isn't associated with work and in a comfortable position that doesn't involve knee or back pain.

The John Bender Way

[Inhale] "Who cares?" [Exhale]

[Inhale, emptying your mind of your to-do list] "Being bad feels pretty good." [Exhale]

[Inhale] "The world is an imperfect place." [Exhale]

[Inhale, visualizing your goal] "Wouldn't I be outstanding in that capacity?" [Exhale]

The Ferris Bueller Method

[Inhale] "I am a righteous dude." [Exhale]

[Inhale, visualizing your goal] "Only the meek get pinched, the bold survive." [Exhale]

[Inhale] "I don't believe in the Beatles, I just believe in me." [Exhale]

[Inhale, visualizing yourself from 1,353 feet above the ground] "Anything is peaceful." [Exhale]

The Joel Goodsen Technique

[Inhale, visualizing your business goal] "I deal in human fulfillment." [Exhale]

[Inhale, clearing your mind of negative thoughts] "Sometimes you gotta say, 'what the fuck.'" [Exhale]

Christian version: [Inhale, clearing your mind of negative thoughts] "Every once in awhile you just got to say, 'what the heck,' and take some chances." [Exhale]

[Inhale, visualizing your desire] "No guilt, no doubts, no fear." [Exhale]

[Inhale] "I am very optimistic. I mean it." [Exhale]

[Inhale] "Freedom brings opportunity, opportunity makes your future." [Exhale]

Play

MONEY-SPENDING LIFE HACKS FOR HUMAN FULFILLMENT

Most Gen Xers have been working for twenty-five to forty years. We all have stories of how we got by in the early years of working through high school, college, and our first job out of college. In high school, I bought a ninety-nine-cent cheese sandwich and used my thirty-two-ounce Subway cup that allowed me to get refills (no ice, please) in perpetuity for twenty-five cents. In college, I wrote checks at the gas station for five dollars because I knew it would take several days to clear the bank and I needed gas to get to my seven dollars per hour job. At my first job out of college, as the director of a conservative nonprofit just outside of Washington, DC, my salary was the equivalent of eleven dollars per hour in one of the highest cost of living cities in America. If I attended a catered event, a can of Diet Coke always made it into my purse on the way out. To save money, I focused on the essentials—food, gas, and Diet Coke.

Over twenty-five years after pocketing those Diet Cokes and accumulating over $50,000 in credit card debt, I am now debt free, saving latchkey retiree money, and spending a little more on products and experiences that make life easier and more enjoyable. If you can afford it, here are my top money-spending hacks. If there's one takeaway on enjoying your Gen X Golden Age, it's to spend like a boomer and think like a millennial.

Rent a Bigger or Newer Car for Road Trips

My common law husband and I are a two-car household and we love our cars—a Mustang GT and a Lexus sedan. Packing for a trip with two adults and one deservedly spoiled cattle dog takes up more space than the average trunk can accommodate. Additionally, our cars aren't new because we love them and—even more importantly—love not having a car payment. For road trips longer than three hours, rent a car that's roomier and possibly more reliable for the long haul than your car. It probably also gets better gas mileage than an older car, if you still have one, like us.

Fly First Class

The first time I ever flew first class it was because of a free upgrade. The second time, I considered it a public service, given that I was over three hundred pounds at the time. If you're a type A person, hate public transportation, and want to cut the stress of flying by 75 percent, I highly recommend flying first class if your budget allows for it. Yes, it's expensive, but so are coach flights once all the fees are added. For domestic flights that are more than three hours long, it's often only a couple hundred dollars more.

My top reasons it's worth it:

- Better person-to-bathroom ratio.
- More seat room, leg room, and elbow room.
- You'll always have overhead room for your stuff.
- Priority service at check-in, on the flight, and baggage claim.
- No checked baggage fees (for bags up to seventy pounds, for many airlines).
- You get to board whenever you want (though I prefer boarding first) and you can get off the plane first.
- Drink and meal service, because not only do they offer more than coach, it helps pass the time.

When I discuss this life hack with friends, I am usually alone in my passion for the value of flying first class, but I will not be peer pressured to go back to coach. My commitment level to first class? I don't even drink alcohol.

Get Groceries Delivered

To gain an extra hour or two in your weekend, get groceries delivered. I tend to get the same staple items, occasionally adding new things seasonally or if they are on sale. If you enjoy the search, there are plenty of ways to do it online by shopping by newest or highest value coupons. Most produce items also allow you to leave a note on ripeness, like specifying what kind of avocados you want. There's nothing like starting Saturday morning with a full fridge, especially while still in pajamas.

Meal Kits

Don't fret if you think you'll miss the lack of inspiration while grocery shopping. My favorite way to seduce the palette and expand my cooking repertoire are meal kits from Blue Apron or HelloFresh. While there may be a money-saving case to be made, that's not why they add enjoyment to life. They help me learn new recipes, new cooking techniques, and cut down on shopping for recipe-specific ingredients. Essentially, it's having a personal shopper and sous chef.

Buy Luxurious, Natural Fabrics

We made it through the polyester, rayon, and whatever chemicals make your shirt change colors era. Leave the fast fashion and its hideous microtrends to the younger generations still trying to find themselves. It's time to splurge on luxurious, natural fabrics, like cashmere, silk, high-quality cotton, and linen, to elevate your style and your quality of life. Natural fabrics offer breathability, regulating body temperature year-round. Silk and cashmere wick moisture, while linen stays crisp and softens over time. Unlike polyester, which pills and fades, cashmere and silk can last decades. Let's make the best of those decades we have left. Their unique textures—silk's sheen, cashmere's softness, linen's relaxed drape—offer elegance that synthetic posers can't match.

Most importantly, don't be precious with these items—use them. Don't let them collect dust like your aunt's Bradford Exchange collection, only to be packed away by her heirs and dropped off at Goodwill or sold in a bundle on eBay. Wear the silk shirt on the weekend with your distressed denim. Bring the cashmere wrap on the plane rather than saving it for a glamorous evening out. These are our living years. Like the perfect leather moto jacket and Rob Lowe, they only get better with age.

Beauty and Spa Treatments

We're the Hawaiian Tropic and baby oil generation. Now we have to pay for it—with spa treatments! Facials and other skin or body treatments are great for avoiding more costly procedures and indulging in some peace and quiet. To preserve your Generation X safe space, find aestheticians and massage therapists who don't ruin the experience with small talk. Avoid weekends, especially in June, when the twenty and thirtysomething bridal parties in the relaxation room begin to gather.

HOW TO RESPOND TO BIG BIRTHDAY OR WEEKEND PLANS QUESTIONS

Do you find yourself dreading the weekend or your birthday because it elicits the question, "Any big plans?"

Remember that you are Generation X and you don't apologize for who you are and how you spend your time. We were expected to entertain ourselves for twelve to fourteen hours per day during the summer. If someone from a younger generation is asking, it's because they haven't learned one of life's most important lessons—the best plans are no plans. That's when the magic happens—finding something epic in the mundane. Like a summer day without cable, there's no limit to what can happen during a weekend with no plans. Maybe a midafternoon, Saturday nap? An evening of homemade popcorn and an old movie? A productive morning of errands and chores? If a boomer is asking, it's because they still think of you as a kid without responsibilities. They may be disappointed by an unexciting answer, but they mean well.

When it comes to birthdays, we were lucky if we got a party, let alone a day. There were no birthday weeks or birthday months. The only memory we have of adult parties are the Over the Hill parties when an adult turned forty. Now we roll our eyes at millennials moaning about turning thirty or forty. Big expectations usually lead to big disappointments. Did New Year's Eve or a trip to New York City ever live up to the hype?

Instead of revealing the freedom of no big plans or satisfaction from being productive, use your Gen X movie memories to answer.

Example One:

> *I was cleaning out the attic at my parents' house last weekend. Unfortunately, it's looking like it's going into foreclosure. Anyway, I found an old painting. It was damaged and I noticed there was a map behind it. It looks like it's to a little, hole-in-the-wall dive that I thought was closed. We're going to check that out. They're supposed to have a good selection of ice cream. By the way, did you hear about that guy who broke out of jail? Apparently, his mom and brother helped him. They sound dangerous.*

Example Two:

> *Some of my friends from childhood are in town. We're going camping, and probably going to do some hiking, too. There are a lot of wild blueberry bushes on the trail. Free, organic blueberries! You just have to watch out for the train tracks that run*

alongside it. We're all kind of going in our separate directions but we could use the bonding time.

Example Three:

I was able to get out of some other commitments so I could spend the day with my significant other and a friend from high school. He recently acquired a vintage Ferrari. We're going to the Art Institute of Chicago, then get some lunch at a French restaurant that's really hard to get into, but we know someone with a reservation. After lunch, we're going to catch a baseball game. Traffic is going to be horrible because there's a parade but we'll make the best of it. Then, I'll probably get in a run before dinner.

Example Four:

I have to do community service because of a minor explosion that happened in my garage. There are some other people in my neighborhood who also have to be there for various reasons. We have nothing in common, so should be a pretty boring day. One guy just blasts whatever sport is on TV on his backyard patio, living out his high school glory days—a real sporto. The neighborhood outcast is also on the list. Who knows what she did? She probably has nothing better to do. Also, the neighborhood princess got a DUI. She just got a divorce and you can tell it won't be too long until she really lets herself go. I'm sure the guy who lives next door to me will be there. The cops gave him a citation for smoking in his backyard. They're out there at least once a week and he doesn't seem to care.

CREATE YOUR OWN DOPAMINE MENU

Beware of generational creep. As our workplace, homes, and social spots get invaded by younger generations, we must be careful to not adopt their habits and customs.

A 2022 study from the *Journal of Student Research* explored how Generation Z's heavy social media use impacts dopamine levels. It found (via Snapchat, of course) that 93 percent of Gen Z are social media users, with 66 percent deeming it vital, averaging one to more than eight hours daily. The study's authors emphasized dopamine's role in their social media use. However, excessive social media use, likened to a "digital drug," may dysregulate dopamine, as "technological advances activate the brain's dopaminergic pathways artificially," potentially causing addiction or mental health issues like depression.

Dr. Anna Lembke, an addiction expert, warns in her book, *Dopamine Nation*, that smartphones are turning us into dopamine junkies, acting as "the modern-day hypodermic needle" for seeking quick hits of attention and validation. It's junk food. She says that constant swipes, likes, and posts fuel behavioral addictions, noting, "We're seeing a huge explosion in the numbers of people struggling with minor addictions." Dopamine, the brain's reward driver, spikes in anticipation and dips post-activity, creating a cycle where "for every high, there is a low." Digital bingeing erodes attention spans and happiness, as "the data shows we're less and less happy" despite endless stimulation.

Your dopamine diet is just as important as your food diet. There's nothing wrong with seeking a hit of dopamine but just say no to digital junk food.

Some ideas for a dopamine menu to dazzle all your senses:

- Cuddle a dog.
- Open and close a Trapper Keeper, savoring the sound.
- Listen to "Relax" by Frankie Goes to Hollywood.
- Get your skis shined up, grab a stick of Juicy Fruit. The taste is going to move you.
- Watch *Magnum, P.I.*

COMBATTING CENSORSHIP, OR HOW TO BUILD YOUR PHYSICAL MEDIA LIBRARY

The Parents Music Resource Center was a group formed in 1985 by a handful of prominent, busybody Washington, DC wives. Tipper Gore (married to then-Senator Al Gore) and others lobbied their husbands to tackle what they saw as a rising tide of objectionable content in popular music—sex, drugs, and rock and roll.

The PMRC kicked off when Tipper bought Prince's *Purple Rain* for her daughter and flipped out over "Darling Nikki." She teamed up with other Washington wives to go after what they called the "porn rock" epidemic. They compiled a "Filthy Fifteen" list. The list is pretty tame by today's standards given that the writer of "WAP (Wet-Ass P***y)" performed at a 2024 Democratic fundraiser.

To protect kids, the PMRC pushed for warning labels—"Parental Advisory: Explicit Content"—on albums, encouraging the music industry to self-regulate. Naturally, the labels were any easy way for Gen X to spot cool music. On Joe Rogan's podcast, rapper and actor Ice Cube said he and NWA leaned into the label's "forbidden fruit" aspect that made albums more appealing. Self-regulating was marketing genius, proving that Washington wives with nothing to do actually did more harm than good (if you are concerned about the "porn rock" epidemic).

Today's PMRC are the woke minority pushing studios and streaming platforms to remove language and scenes from film and television classics they deem problematic. Among the movies and TV shows that have been edited:

> *Gone with the Wind* (1939), for racial depictions
>
> *Dumbo* (1941), for reference to Jim Crow laws and depicting racial stereotypes (though not removed, a warning was added about content)
>
> *The French Connection* (1971), for racial language
>
> *Grease* (1978), for suggestive language
>
> *Revenge of the Nerds* (1984), for lack of consent
>
> *Sixteen Candles* (1984), for depicting date rape
>
> *The Breakfast Club* (1985), for homophobic locker graffiti
>
> *Crocodile Dundee* (1986), for transphobia
>
> *Adventures in Babysitting* (1987), for homophobic language
>
> *Aladdin* (1992), for stereotypical depictions of Arabs

Home Alone 2: Lost in New York (1992) in some broadcasts, because cameo of Orange Man is bad

Toy Story 2 (1999), for a casting couch joke

Episodes of *30 Rock*, *Community*, *The Office* (American), and *It's Always Sunny in Philadelphia* for featuring blackface

Physical media—DVDs, Blu-rays, and even VHS tapes—inoculate your memories from the woke busybodies of today. Physical media matters because it gives you tangible ownership of your favorite movies and shows, free from the fears and whims of streaming services or corporate edits. Unlike digital copies, which can vanish when a platform loses rights or decides to tweak content, a disk on your shelf stays yours, unalterable by anyone. It's a bulwark against censorship, preserving films as they were meant to be seen, complete with special features like commentaries and director's cuts.

Physical copies, though, can also get hit. Studios have released edited versions on disk before, sometimes unmarked. eBay is your best bet for finding original versions. Always be sure to check that it's a version compatible with US players.

Censorship isn't always blatant bans; it's often subtle trims or removals driven by cultural shifts, corporate PR, or legal pressure. Preserve your memories of the classics—problematic jokes and all—by grabbing your favorites while you can.

THINGS YOU'RE TOO OLD TO DO

While I hesitate to limit the possibilities in our new Golden Age, there are some things that Gen Xers simply shouldn't do any longer for their own good or for the good of their family and friends:

- Ask a friend to help you move.
- Ask a friend to pick you up at the airport (significant others and family are okay).
- Send nude pics.
- Fight with strangers on the internet (yes, that includes neighborhood groups).
- Have a hangover.
- Expect someone to do work for free or for "exposure."
- Expect a professional like a lawyer, doctor, or mechanic to give you free advice.
- Not go to the doctor after an injury.
- Be in debt (aside from your mortgage).
- Have anything pierced other than your ears.

- Ask to crash on a friend or family member's couch because you don't want to pay for a hotel (being offered a guest room is okay).
- Use a backpack for work.
- Sleep on a mattress not in a frame.
- Participate in a TikTok challenge.
- Show up empty-handed to a party.
- Not finish a prescription, despite doctor's orders.

THINGS YOU'RE *NOT* TOO OLD TO DO

The purpose of this book is to remind you that "middle age" is only the halfway point, or—better yet—a starting point for a better life. You might have more time than you used to before kids and other life commitments. Remember what Miles from *Risky Business* said—"Freedom brings opportunity, opportunity makes your future."

- Fall in love again or for the first time
- Change careers
- Become debt-free
- Improve your health
- Open an IRA
- Write a bestselling book (fingers crossed…)
- Create the body you always wanted
- Immerse yourself in a new hobby
- Be saved
- Buy something expensive because you love it and can afford it

- Use Instagram filters if it makes you feel good
- Give up a bad habit
- Untether yourself from people and places that don't make you a better human

Style

THE TWO RETRO METHOD

Imagine boarding a "fashion train," where the decade you choose to exit becomes the one that defines your style forever. Once you step off, your personal look is locked into the clothing trends of that era, regardless of what's fashionable now.

For example, if you get off at the "1970s" stop, you'd be committed to wearing things like wide collared shirts and flared pants for men, or long skirts and platform shoes for women—stuck in that decade's aesthetic no matter the current year (at the time of writing this, several of these items are currently trends).

Gen Xers pride themselves on not looking like they raided Barry Manilow's wardrobe. We want to wear the styles we like, regardless of trends. But we don't want to look like a prepackaged Spirit Halloween 80s Party Girl or Punk Rock Music Guy costume. That's why the Two Retro Method should be your style guide.

The Two Retro Method is only wearing two items of clothing or accessories that are vintage or vintage-inspired (important reminder: pre-2000 is now considered "vintage"). For example, one off-the-shoulder sweatshirt plus one pair of leggings equals an outfit. One off the shoulder sweatshirt plus one pair of leggings plus one pair of classic pumps equals 80s Flashy Dancer Icon costume.

An example for him: one vintage concert shirt plus one blazer with scrunched sleeves equals outfit. One vintage concert shirt plus one blazer with scrunch sleeves plus one white pleated pants equals South Beach Undercover Vice Cop.

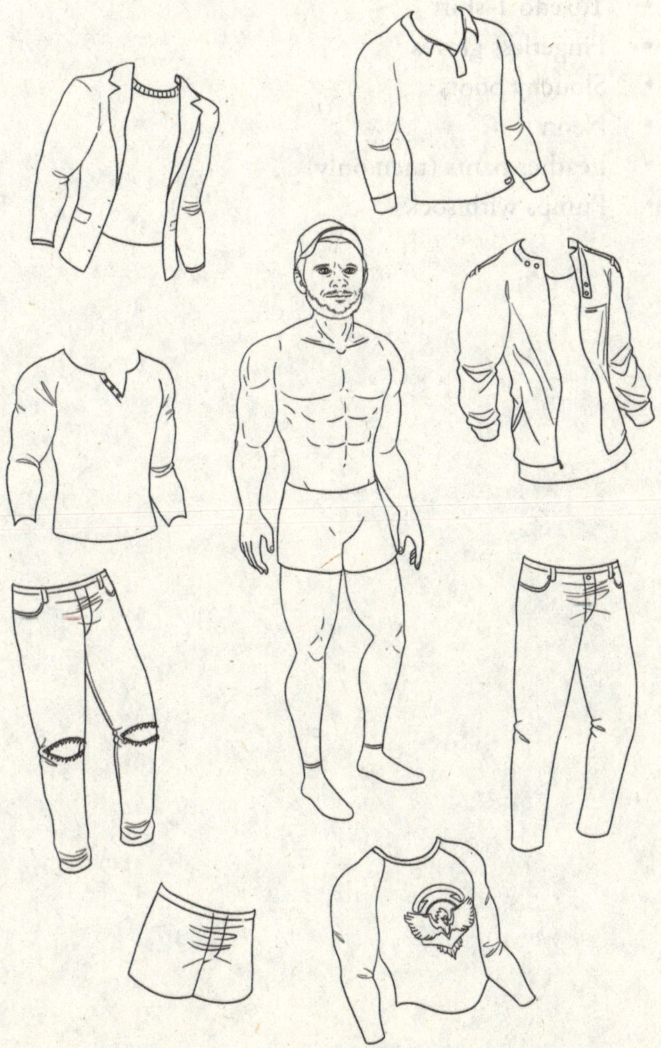

The exceptions to this rule are iconic pieces that can carry a look on their own, such as:

- Members Only racing jacket
- Amanda Peterson's suede outfit
- Tuxedo T-shirt
- Fingerless gloves
- Slouchy boots
- Neon
- Leather pants (men only)
- Pumps with socks

IS BUYING DISTRESSED SELLING OUT?

Today's younger generations may never understand the satisfaction of getting a pair of jeans perfectly worn in and earning its distressed look, cutting a sweatshirt that eventually hangs perfectly, or that band T-shirt that's so soft it's almost see-through. Now you can buy pre-distressed jeans and pre-cut muscle Ts and sweatshirts. You certainly can't blame them for buying our (or our parents') band T-shirts. A Led Zeppelin, Ramones or Van Halen T-shirt will be cool forever. I won't even pretend to know what bands are cool now. I know it's not the Jonas Brothers. Or are they doing a reunion tour now for aughts nostalgia?

Buying distressed isn't necessarily selling out, but you do lose the authenticity factor. It doesn't make someone a poser, but it robs them of the experience of earning the rips, distress, and comfort. It's no surprise that younger generations seek instant gratification rather than the pleasure of the moment when a stiff free shirt becomes as soft as cashmere. It's also part of being human when you experience the anguish of losing your favorite T-shirt (I know you took my José Cuervo Spring Break 1991 T-shirt, Jennifer).

Likewise, buying an item with your favorite brand of cigarettes, soda, or snack isn't the same as earning it the old-fashioned way with Camel Cash or being the first hundred people in line at a store opening. You couldn't just buy a Ford or Budweiser shirt at Target. There was a limited supply, and wearing it signaled your commitment to the brand. You were willing to save points, stand in line, or flirt with a semi-employed radio DJ to get that free T-shirt.

Buying distressed isn't selling out—it's simply lazy, and you're better than that. Patience is among the traits that made us a stronger, more resilient generation.

CHEAT CODES FOR LOOKING YOUNGER

Plastic surgery and expensive med spa visits aren't the only way to retain your youth and look more attractive. As the countdown begins to retirement, we're in the final stretch to boost our nest eggs during the Golden Age. A study published in the *American Economic Review* in 1994 analyzed data from the US and Canada, and found that people rated as above average in attractiveness earned about 10 to 15 percent more than those rated below average, even when controlling for factors like education and experience. This makes the attractiveness gap more real than the phony wage gap between women and men.

In the book, *Beauty Pays*, one of the prior study's researchers, Daniel Hamermesh, wrote, "Over a lifetime, an attractive worker in the United States might earn $230,000 more than an unattractive one, even with similar education and experience."

Of course, this isn't purely for being more attractive. Hamermesh noted, "Better-looking people often develop greater self-confidence because of how others treat them, and this confidence can translate into better performance in job interviews, negotiations, and workplace interactions.

A big part of what society views as attractive are qualities of youth—energy and vitality, smooth skin, shiny hair, and overall physical fitness. The key for Generation X is to combine this knowledge and practice with our independent and aloof attitude. Here are some cheat codes that require minimal effort to maximize your earning potential.

Bangs

In July 2013, AdWeek's FishbowlDC Summer Superlatives generously awarded me the title of Best Bangs. Since then, I've extoled the virtues of bangs, especially as I've gotten older. From Bettie Page and Joan Jett, to Audrey Hepburn and Debbie Harry, bangs have helped hide fine lines and effects of a late night and early morning. In addition to being cheaper than Botox, bangs are a chic, low commitment way to refresh a hairstyle and take emphasis off your forehead. For round faces, choppy or long, center parted bangs elongate the face. Square faces benefit from sideswept or tapered bangs to soften the jawline. Heart shaped faces are balanced with long, tapered, or sideswept bangs. Oval faces offer versatility, with longer bangs recommended for longer ovals to add width. Bangs are a fun, (eventually) reversible choice to tell the world that you prefer the frustration of an oddly placed cowlick over needles. Did I mention they're also cheaper than Botox?

Sunglasses

Sunglasses are magic—they make you look younger while also protecting you from aging. They project a youthful, "too cool for school" appearance with style and practicality. They conceal wrinkles and unsightly undereye bags with larger or wraparound lenses. Tinted or polarized lenses brighten the face, diverting attention from tired eyes. Bold, trendy frames like, oversized or funky shapes, boost confidence, signaling a modern, energetic vibe. Angular, classic frames like Wayfarers sharpen the jawline, countering sagging, while rectangular ones define rounder faces. Playful designs, such as bright colors or retro styles, evoke a carefree, youthful spirit. Choose frames suiting your face shape—oval faces are versatile, square faces soften with round lenses—and opt for quality classics like matte black Wayfarers or tortoiseshell Aviators for timeless appeal. The added bonus is UV protection. Sunglasses also help prevent squinting and sun exposure from further damage.

A Healthy Tan

For Generation X and older generations, a tan has been associated with health. Previously associated with labor while pale skin was a sign of wealth, the Skin Cancer Foundation, among other sources, said the change happened in the 1920s when Coco Chanel got sunburned on a trip in the Mediterranean. Her bronze glow set the trend for a tan as a sign of health and leisure. In modern times, the association continues because of those old vibes—leisure, vitality, and natural radiance—mixed with a modern fitness culture that prizes an "active lifestyle" look. Social media perpetuates the image as filters and influencers keep the bronzed ideal alive. Vitamin D is an important benefit of sun exposure, but the days of slathering on baby oil and getting a "base tan" are over. There are many self-tanning products on the market and they've come a long way since the days of orange streaks and that telltale smell. Just remember to exfoliate and use sparingly on knees and elbows.

Makeup to Enhance Minimal Makeup Look

Every season, the beauty influencer community has a new name for the "no makeup" makeup look—clean girl aesthetic, glass skin, monochrome minimalism, flushed look, soft glam, just to name a few. The key is to wear makeup that enhances your best features and looks flawless. Think bridal makeup that takes less than fifteen minutes. The base for any good makeup look is good skin—that's where you should spend your time and money. For makeup, even if your preference is for full coverage foundation, opt for products like highlighter, bronzer, and blush to avoid the pancake look and add color. For eyes, go minimal and avoid the young influencer, complicated eyeshadow looks, like *Euphoria*-inspired glitter, graphic liner and bold eyeshadow.

Generation X men, I speak to you now: if you're looking for a manly glow up, you need to take care of your skin, too. No more Irish Spring or Dial as body, shampoo, and face wash. You should also use tinted moisturizer to even out tone or just under your eyes. Don't fret about it not being masculine. You think you're more manly than Glenn Danzig or Prince just because you don't wear makeup? As if.

AVOID CLOTHING THAT ADVERTISES COMFORT FIRST

We've reached the age when function is marketed to us over style. Some key words and phrases to avoid:

- Slip-on
- Relaxed
- Comfortable
- Move with ease
- Supportive
- Breathable
- Feel the difference
- Cozy fit
- Flexible
- Stretchy
- Adjustable band

Instead, wear clothes that fit your style and body that happen to be comfortable. No Velcro, ever.

DRESS LIKE MUSK, NOT FETTERMAN

A Gallup poll found, "The vast majority of US workers wear casual clothes on the job most days, with more than seven in [ten] saying their typical workplace attire is business casual (41 [percent]) or more dressed down, casual street clothes (31 [percent]). Another 23 [percent] of workers say they wear a uniform at work most days, while just 3 [percent] say wearing business professional clothes is their norm."

Consider this—that 3 percent isn't necessarily a US senator! The media often describes Senator John Fetterman as dressing like the everyday man and with "working-class energy." Is this what reporters think we working class dress like for work? It's a total disconnect with who the everyday man and woman are. Most people who work outside of the office opt for business casual on most days, while some do dress in suits and corporate attire. Fetterman is the sloppy, lovable minority.

Elon Musk is a good example of a Gen Xer who embraces business casual quirkiness but knows when an occasion calls for more formal attire, like a suit at a joint session of Congress or a tuxedo for a red-carpet event.

As pop culture icon Donald Trump said, "[Elon Musk] has some very brilliant young people working for him that dress much worse than him actually—they dress in just [T]-shirts. You wouldn't know they have 180 IQ."

Expectations are low and it doesn't take much to stand out.

Love and Family

THE RULES ACCORDING TO JOHN HUGHES

Beginning in the 1980s and reaching a fever pitch in the 1990s, the pickup artists took over the dating scene. These self-proclaimed gurus included pickup artist pioneer Ross Jeffries and "Mystery," a Canadian magician turned dating coach. In his books, Jeffries preached not to chase but to attract. His "Speed Seduction" rules for men emphasize psychological tactics over traditional dating. He told men to use suggestive storytelling to spark attraction, avoid chasing by projecting confidence, and evoke emotions like curiosity with phrases like "Have you ever felt…?" To encourage these feelings, men should stay unpredictable, anchor positive feelings to yourself, and maintain emotional independence. It was about mindset and control, not actions.

The response from relationship gurus for women was *The Rules: Time-tested Secrets for Capturing the Heart of Mr. Right*, written by Ellen Fein and Sherrie Schneider. It quickly gained popularity throughout the late 1990s, becoming a cultural phenomenon. The book offered women a set of thirty-five dating rules to follow to attract and marry their ideal partner, emphasizing traditional gender roles and strategic behavior. Its rise was fueled by media coverage, word-of-mouth, and its appeal to women seeking a structured approach to dating.

Among the popular rules:

- Don't Accept a Saturday Night Date after Wednesday
- Don't See Him More Than Once or Twice a Week
- Don't Call Him and Rarely Return His Calls

Women were taught to be elusive creatures that the men pursued; we were to appeal to his hunter instincts. It's a miracle anyone ever coupled up, especially once "Mystery" and the later pickup artists introduced concepts like "negging"—a subtle insult so the target starts to seek your approval. For example, "You could be a real knockout if you tried a little harder."

Thankfully, Gen X already had a base knowledge for how romantic relationships formed and flourished. Filmmaker John Hughes taught us the birds and the bees between the geeks and the "richies." He was our relationship guru, and we grew up seeing love through his lens. By the time Gen Xers arrived in middle or high school, we embraced the rules according to John Hughes.

Opposites Attract

One constant scenario presented to Generation Xers was that opposites attract: the shy, quirky girl is secretly in love with the popular boy; the rich boy is captivated by the poor girl; or the good girl is strangely attracted to the bad boy. This taught us to look outside our cliques and social networks for love. For those still looking for love, look outside the dating apps.

Enemies Become Friends

The Breakfast Club is the classic example of enemies, like Claire and Allison or Brian and everyone else, finding common ground despite being enemies. They find shared vulnerabilities and pressures despite their financial and social differences. Likewise, in *Ferris Bueller's Day Off*, Jeanne helps Ferris evade Principal Rooney because he is their common enemy. In modern love for Gen Xers, there are enemies everywhere: the Karen on the neighborhood Facebook group, the homeowner association, or cashiers who can't make change. Connect with the person who may have once left their trash can out too long to talk trash about the Karen who complained about your yard while you were on vacation. Share a loud conversation, a drink, and some music with that person within earshot of Karen until 9:01 p.m., as she stews and monitors the time.

It's Okay to Be a Late Bloomer

Before the "nice guy" was tarnished by feminist bloggers, they were the ones we rooted for in movies. In the John Hughes universe, they were the outsiders, misfits, and late bloomers. They were Keith, Cameron, and Duckie. They were the ones who believed in love even from the sidelines. Their intentions were pure, and by the end of the movie, they made the right decision. It doesn't matter if you're behind in a timeline set by someone else, we're all in charge of the course we set for love and other milestones we want to achieve. As Cameron said, "I am not going to sit on my ass as the events that affect me unfold to determine the course of my life. I'm going to take a stand. I'm going to defend it. Right or wrong, I'm going to defend it."

Friends Become Lovers

Every boy or girl who connected with *Some Kind of Wonderful* held out hope that his or her best friend would one day feel the same way. Susan Watts was the stereotypical female friend—tough but vulnerable, loyal to her friend, funny, and not like other girls. Keith was the stereotypical male friend—unlucky in love, shy, sweet, and totally clueless about how Watts felt.

If you're still looking for the kiss that kills, consider your single friends. Is there someone who never hesitates to offer to pick you up at the airport? Is there someone who is perfect aside from your irrational "must be over six feet" rule? Give that friend who has always been there for you a second look. As Watts said, "Don't go mistaking paradise for a pair of long legs."

The fantasy that every funny or chubby or quirky Gen Xer had—that the crush/best friend would one day feel the same way—happened to me. I fell in love with my best friend and he fell in love with me. Like Watts said at the end of the movie, "I hoped. I didn't know."

ACT LIKE TEENAGERS TO REKINDLE THE ROMANCE

After high school, many Gen Xers' dating life was filled with the angst and awkwardness of the 1990s. We were still pre-internet but tech was starting to creep in with answering machines and AOL chatrooms. Our late high school/early college dating was shaped by movies like *Singles*. It nailed the quiet, introspective side of Gen X. We still had our rebellious side but we were now searching for connection in a world that felt increasingly disconnected. Of course, now people are more disconnected than ever! *Singles* was a time capsule of a specific era of music, coffee shops, and the feeling that adulthood arrived too fast.

Our angst is now about the future. The best way to take a break from it and rekindle the romance with your partner is to go back to the past. This is particularly fun if the two of you met later in life.

Take a Walk

In middle and high school, the time spent with your crush walking from locker to class or home from the bus stop was the highlight of the day. Maximize the romantic connection by banning adult problem conversations (money, the to-do list, kids, for example) during these walks.

Make Out to Your Middle School Dance Playlist

Burned into our brains are those mandatory school dances the last few periods of school. Girls and boys stood in groups until a select few paired up. Over the loudspeaker in the gym, we heard ballads from Chicago, REO Speedwagon, Bad English, and the king of the love ballads, Bryan Adams.

To jumpstart your heart, here are some classics to get you in the mood to get felt up over the bra, under the blouse, hoping to God your children don't walk in.

"If You Leave" by Orchestral Manoeuvres in the Dark
"Open Arms" by Journey
"Heaven" by Bryan Adams
"Eternal Flame" by The Bangles
"I Want to Know What Love Is" by Foreigner
"Glory of Love" by Peter Cetera
"Can't Fight This Feeling Anymore" by REO Speedwagon
"Patience" by Guns N' Roses
"Right Here Waiting" by Richard Marx
"Time After Time" by Cyndi Lauper

"(Everything I Do) I Do It For You" by Bryan Adams
"You're the Inspiration" by Chicago
"Crazy for You" by Madonna
"When I See You Smile" by Bad English
"Straight From the Heart" by Bryan Adams
"Broken Wings" by Mr. Mister
"Keep on Loving You" by REO Speedwagon
"Against All Odds (Take a Look at Me Now)" by Phil Collins
"Take My Breath Away" by Berlin
"Don't You (Forget About Me)" by Simple Minds

Practice Vintage Values

MTV icon and Fox News host Rachel Campos-Duffy said, "As the events [and] problems in our country become increasingly out of our control, the more I embrace the spiritual significance of the beauty, warmth and life in my home. I draw even closer to my family, our ancient traditions, [and] our faith. The things that last."

As a trad common-law wife, I couldn't agree more. Practicing vintage values, like eating dinner together, making a home together, and even starting new family traditions, reinforces your family unit. It can be a family with two parents and nine kids or a family of two and a cattle dog named Cora.

THE JOY OF WATCHING RERUNS

Many Generation Xers met their partners in college or later in life at work or in social circles outside their hometowns. While we share the same experiences with pop culture, we didn't experience them together. Now with some life experience under our belts, like bullies who never made it out of their hometown, jerk bosses, heartache, and knowledge that the head cheerleader gained fifty pounds, we can rewatch some of the seventies and eighties classics as adults and appreciate them on a deeper level, especially the very special episodes—and by that, I mean make snide comments and observations to one another until we hit the sheets at 9:00 p.m. It's *Mystery Science Theater 3000* with the one you love.

Some shows I appreciate even more the second and third time around:

Dallas
Dynasty
Family Ties
The Golden Girls
The Larry Sanders Show

Magnum, P.I.
Miami Vice
The Rockford Files
Roseanne

COMBINING YOUR COLLECTIONS

Two adults moving in together is a lot different when you're a decade or two past your college years. You both now have quality furniture you bought (rather than picked up off the side of the road), a style you prefer, and a few collections you enjoy displaying. So, what do you do when a minimalist falls in love with a maximalist? When he's mid-century modern and she's Regency Moderne? Luckily, Gen Xers have a lot of the same pop culture experiences and the same visceral reaction to the boomer aesthetic, now embraced ironically by younger millennials and Gen Z. You won't find any geese in the kitchen or sunflowers in the bedroom in our homes. We're so over it.

Our furniture and collections reflect our eclectic blend of new or rescued mid-century modern pieces, eighties and nineties tchotchkes, and quirky memorabilia. Combining these into a cohesive space is about balancing nostalgia with practicality.

Use Mid-century Modern Basics as Anchors

Use furniture like a credenza, a low-slung sofa with tapered legs, or a Danish-style chair as the foundation. Their clean lines and timeless appeal ground the room. Keep upholstery neutral (gray, tan, navy) to let bolder items pop.

Layer in Unique Pieces

Integrate that chunky oak coffee table or a kitschy lighting fixture. Pair it with a collection—say, a stack of vinyl records displayed on a shelf or a complete set of McDonald's eighties-era glasses. The key is intentional curation; don't overcrowd. Pick a few standout pieces and give them breathing room.

Mix Textures and Colors

Gen X loves bold—think MTV-era brights. Toss a rug under that sleck mid-century sofa, combine it with a draped a blanket over a retro armchair to bring all the pieces together. Whatever you do, don't buy the as-seen-in-showroom furniture set.

Mix and Display Your Collections

Vintage Pyrex dishes or movie memorabilia can double as decor on open shelves, adding pops of color without clashing. It's also fun to mix your stuff together so it looks like a home you've made together and not like a store display.

Functional Nostalgia

Make it livable. You don't want to be the person telling a visitor not to open the box or to put on gloves before handling. If you have those items, keep them in a room visitors, especially children, don't peruse. Blend the sentimental with the useful so it's not just a museum.

Contrast Styles Thoughtfully

If you have a minimalist mid-century table but a loud collection of concert tees, frame a few shirts in a simple metal or black frame as art to bridge the gap. Avoid chaos by sticking to a loose color palette (such as, retro oranges, greens, and browns) or a theme (music, movies, tech). The vibe should feel like a Gen X time capsule—irreverent yet intended. Picture a room where a sleek Eames knockoff sits next to a Garfield phone, with a turntable spinning the Ramones. It's not about perfection, it's about personality and authenticity. To build a solid relationship, you need the freedom to lean into her maximalism's excess and pare it back with his mid-century's restraint. You have to find the balance to mix his collection of movie posters and her collection of art from the set of *Mad Men*.

THE ONE TRICK TO RAISING RESILIENT, INDEPENDENT KIDS

There is one difference between the way we grew up in the 1980s and how post-2000 children grew up that holds the key for raising resilient, independent kids: ***kids must be made to ride the school bus.***

Riding a school bus in the 1980s and earlier was *Lord of the Flies* on wheels—equal parts chaos, camaraderie, and kids left to fend for themselves. The chaos started as soon as the bell rang. Around a circular driveway was a fleet of orange-yellow buses. The smell of diesel was in the air. Kids had what felt like three to five minutes to find their ride home based on small numbers in a different place on each bus. If a bus was being serviced, which was often, you hoped there was a handwritten sign with the bus number in the window. A fancy school may have had someone with a clipboard with the bus number code but good luck finding him before the bus took off. The bus driver didn't do a headcount or announce what bus you were on. She didn't care where you got off and what happened to you before that.

For a lot of Gen X kids, the bus ride was a daily ritual, a noisy bridge between school and freedom. The seats were covered in green or brown vinyl that stuck to your legs in the heat and cracked over time. Duct tape patched up a couple areas, others left open to reveal there was absolutely no cushion. Safety standards were looser back then—do I even need to mention there were no seatbelts? Kids bounced around like balls in a Fisher-Price Corn Popper toy vacuum when the bus hit a pothole or went down a dirt road.

Some drivers let kids crank up a radio, toss a football down the aisle, or hang out the windows as long as no one got hurt—or at least admitted it. Some drivers ignored the chatter and horseplay, treating the bus like a rolling playground. They'd only step in if things got too rowdy, like if a fight broke out. But what power did they have? Did you ever hear about someone getting suspended for anything done on a school bus? It was them versus up to fifty kids. At most, they'd shout, "Sit down!" or "Knock it off!" through the big rearview mirror, but enforcement was spotty. It wasn't worth the battle. For them, it was a race to get to the final stop and to the end of the shift.

Seating was its own hierarchy. Older kids claimed the back, where they could goof off out of the driver's sight, while the front was for the ones who wanted to stay out of sight of the older kids and in sight of the driver.

You dreaded being late and having last pick at seats. For a chubby kid like me, the prospect of a quiet, uneventful ride got worse the further you had to walk back into the bus. Kids in the back, out of sight, ran wild—swapping seats, yelling across the aisle, sitting the cool way, facing out rather than straight ahead. There was an unspoken rule that they wouldn't pick on you if you moved as soon as there was an empty seat closer to the front. Until then, you were on your own, hugging your stuff into your body so nothing was dropped and lost forever. There were no phones to distract the bullies. You only had your wits, or candy to share, if you were lucky. The experience led to resilience in uncomfortable situations.

The miserable school bus experience was also a motivator to get a driver's license, a job, and a car. Learning to drive was the spark that lights the fire of independence.

The light seems to be fading for younger generations. Data from the Federal Highway Administration shows a significant decline in the percentage of teenagers obtaining licenses. In 1983, about 46 percent of sixteen-year-olds in the United States had a driver's license. By 2020, that number dropped to around 25 percent.

It's time to bring back the bus ride experience. No more school pick-up line or Uber teen accounts—teach those kids to seek independence and a better life.

For extra credit, make them drink from the hose during the summer and go to a community college for their first two years.

(P.S. I'm on to all of you parents in the school pick up line. I know you're just using it as an excuse to come into work late and leave work early!)

THE WEIRD SCIENCE OF AI PARENTING: WHAT TO DO WITH THESE LITTLE MANIACS

Since we've exhausted my parenting advice, this childless Gen Xer is also open to modern parenting techniques. Like many childless Gen Xers, I generally only see my friends' kids on their Shutterfly Christmas cards. These curated vignettes clash with the short conversations we had on the phone, in which I repeated every sentence and she heard every third word. My friends' well-meaning tips were a mess of contradictions, filtered through their own kid-induced battle scars.

Meanwhile, parenting books came off either too smug or outdated. They were more of a boomer relic, though there was some resurgence with crunchy millennial manifestos with baby food recipes and organic cotton diaper tips.

AI parenting is modern with no judgment, just a soulless artificial brainiac sifting through data. Is it cheating? Yes, but so is ordering a pizza, watching TV with kids, and calling it babysitting.

I asked three AI models to "give me your best parenting advice for Gen Xers with teenagers in 150 words." Here's what our future caretakers said:

From Grok:

> For Gen X parents navigating the wild ride of raising teens in 2025, lean into your strengths: resilience and adaptability. First, set clear boundaries—teens crave structure even if they push back. Consistency is key; follow through on consequences without turning into a dictator. Second, listen more than you lecture. They're drowning in digital noise, so your undivided attention is gold. Ask open-ended questions and resist the urge to fix everything—let them stumble and learn. Third, model balance. Show them how to unplug from screens and prioritize real-world connections, something Gen Xers instinctively get from pre-digital days. Fourth, don't shy away from tough talks—mental health, sex, drugs—but keep it real, not preachy. Finally, cut yourself some slack. You're not perfect, and they don't need you to be—just present. They'll remember your effort more than your flaws. You've got this.

From ChatGPT:

> Gen X parents raising teens should balance structure with independence. Set clear boundaries

but allow room for autonomy. Communication is key—listen without judgment, ask open-ended questions, and avoid lecturing. Understand t hat social media and technology shape their world; engage with it rather than fight it.

Encourage resilience by letting them face natural consequences and solve problems on their own. Model emotional intelligence—show them how to handle stress, apologize when needed, and express feelings constructively. Keep humor alive; laughter eases tension and builds connection.

Prioritize quality time, even if it's just car rides or late-night talks. Teach financial literacy, critical thinking, and adaptability to prepare them for an uncertain future. Support their passions, even if they differ from your own. Most importantly, be a safe, steady presence—your teenager may push away, but they still need your love, guidance, and unwavering support.

From Gemini:

Gen X parents, your teens are navigating a hyperconnected world unlike your own. Prioritize open, honest communication, even when it's uncomfortable. Listen actively, validate their feelings, and resist the urge to immediately solve every problem. Encourage critical thinking, media literacy, and healthy digital habits. Balance independence with boundaries, fostering responsibility and resilience. Remember your own teenage angst? Empathy is key. Let them make mistakes, but offer guidance and support to learn from them. Ultimately, show them unconditional love and be their steady anchor in a rapidly changing world.

GEN XERS NEVER SAY DIE

Gen Xers experienced grief early thanks to pop culture. Every Gen Xer was affected by the death of a character they loved—Optimus Prime, Bambi's mom, Spock in *Star Trek II: The Wrath of Khan*, E.T., Old Yeller, Goose from *Top Gun*, Johnny and Dally from *The Outsiders*, Bobby Ewing from *Dallas*, and, of course, Atreyu's horse, Artax from *The Neverending Story*.

Death wasn't just in movies: we also watched the *Challenger* explosion in the classroom.

We're getting older. The worst part is, so are the people we love.

In November 2016, I was at a friend's house in Rehoboth Beach, Delaware. The election was over, my candidate had won, and it was the beginning of a three-day weekend. My friend and I had spent the day shopping and walking along the boardwalk. It was sunny and in the 60s, pleasant enough for a mid-November birthday weekend in Delaware. It was nearly bedtime when I got a text from Walter, a guy I knew through Floyd, my best friend.

"Did you hear?" he wrote.

"About what?" I wrote back.

"Floyd."

That this conversation was happening was such a coincidence, because the night before it, I had dreamed about Floyd and had woken up remembering it had been a few weeks since we had talked. I woke up thinking it was odd that I hadn't heard from him on my birthday; he usually called or sent flowers.

"No, what happened?" I asked.

"Just received a call. Floyd passed away," he answered.

I immediately went into the guest bedroom and closed the door. At first, I insisted it was a mistake, because Floyd's father was also named Floyd. Maybe someone just got confused. Unfortunately, that wasn't the case. My Floydie had died. I left the beach the next morning and spent the next twenty-four hours crying and unable to sleep.

I first met Floyd in 2003 at an airport. He was working as a bodyguard for a famous author that I often traveled with when she did college speeches. Over the next couple years, Floyd and I traveled together with various speakers, talking about life and politics backstage or while the client did book signings. After my employment at the speaker's bureau ended, we stayed in touch, continued to work together at various events, and would talk on the phone for hours.

A week after I learned of Floyd's death, I drove to Long Beach, New York for his funeral. I had driven to New York before, but always had Floyd's help along on the way. Depending on the time of day, he would text me to take this bridge rather than that bridge, or to check in on where I was and what the traffic was like. If going to Fox News, he would remind me to tell the cab Sixth Avenue instead of Avenue of the Americas so I didn't sound like a tourist. This time my phone remained silent. I had never felt more alone and lost than I did during that drive.

At the funeral, I saw the people I had heard him talk about over the years—his sister, his father, his niece, his former NYPD partner, and fellow bodyguards. I sat with his famous client who had introduced me to him more than a decade before.

Floydie was a solid boomer and preferred talking on the phone instead of text or email. In one of the last email exchanges we had, I told him about an artist I had hired for a work project. In addition to graphic design, he was also a colorist for Marvel and DC Comics and lived in Arizona. Since I was in Arizona for work, I met up with him and couldn't wait to tell Floydie about my friend who worked on Superman. I wrote to him that, "We only talked for an hour or so, but I feel like I've known him for [one hundred] years."

Floyd, the biggest Superman fan I've ever known, wrote back, "That's more than cool. I think you should marry him!" (Nearly ten years later, I did, in the eyes of Texas common law.)

A fresh flood of tears still come when I think of that email. He had said he still displayed the birthday card I had given him a few years ago. When he opened it, it played the *Superman* theme, although he said now it sounded like a tortured animal since the battery was dying.

At the funeral, a family friend read a poem she wrote for Floydie.

He always came out on top
In everything he'd do
He never had a doubt he'd make it through
If anyone could beat this
We thought surely Floydie can
He always made it through before

Cause he was Superman

—Shared by his sister, Becky Resnick Calabrese, excerpted from a poem written by Joann Prisco Fox

Several months before he died, Floyd wrote to me, "I feel like an aging 1979 Trans Am. Great car in its day, but didn't keep up with the maintenance the last 10 years or so and now everything is starting to go!"

Losing someone you love hits hard for anyone, but for Gen Xers it can carry a unique sting as we start to lose our peers. We're at that age where mortality starts creeping into the conversation, but we're also juggling work and family. When someone dies, our first thoughts go to the last time we talked or if we should have done more to reach out. In his song, "Hello, Friend," actor and songwriter James Woods wrote and Shooter Jennings sang:

Hello, friend
I forgot to say goodbye
Slipped my mind
And I don't know why

Thought you'd always be there
And I never feared death
One day I called
You were gone in a breath

It's important to feel the loss; don't just shove it down. We grew up with a "deal with it" vibe, but stuffing emotions just delays the mess. Unresolved grief can spike anxiety and depression, especially in midlife when stress is already high. Cry, scream into a pillow, or blast sad or angry songs.

Talk about it with people who get it. A 2023 study in *Psychology and Aging* found peer support cuts isolation in grief by 40 percent for middle-aged adults. Skip the platitudes and swap stories instead. "Remember when he called us his white trash family on the way to Six Flags?" beats "He's in a better place" every time.

Don't expect a timeline. Grief's not a VHS you can fast-forward. Some days you're fine; others, you're gut punched by a reminder that you can't share good news with him.

My friend Robert Davi, who played bad guy Jake Fratelli in *Goonies*, wrote, "Death is the common enemy we all share[—] knowing this we should all just lift each other up."

Finally, cut yourself slack. You might be the "strong one" for others, but midlife's already a grind. Nap, eat a burger, skip the gym guilt, check your dopamine menu. Self-care's not selfish when you're mourning.

I'll miss you forever, Floydie. I hope your Boop made you proud.

Work

HOW TO STOP BEING WORK MOMMY AND RAISE LATCHKEY EMPLOYEES

Our independence, adaptability, and skepticism of authority shaped our childhood as latchkey kids. As Carla flatly says in *Vision Quest*, "I've been twenty-one since I was fourteen." This mentality now shapes our behavior in the workplace. We value efficiency and self-reliance, and prefer independent work over collaborative efforts. Like our parents, our bosses were boomers and expected our self-reliance and independence. These traits now drive our decisions and expectations at work. One of my favorite compliments a boomer reference gave my eventual boomer boss was, "You only have to tell her to do something once."

Now I want the same from coworkers and employees. My patience lasts as long as the flavor of Fruit Stripe gum.

CNBC reported that in 2024, a survey of 1,500 Gen Zers revealed that 25 percent have brought parents to job interviews. We are quick to criticize the Gen Zer. What about the parent who agreed to come along? Unfortunately, many of the latchkey kids became helicopter parents or work mommy, allowing younger employees to be less self-sufficient and unable to manage their time effectively at work. We only have ourselves and their teachers to blame.

If you have younger millennial or Gen Z coworkers or employees, this chapter will help you empower them to be independent, latchkey employees who can work without constant oversight.

Show Them How Small Tasks Support Large Goals

Many younger millennials and Gen Z employees didn't have jobs in high school. They aren't accustomed to dead-end, tedious work, so when they feel they're in that position, it can be scary. Afterall, they are adults who seek praise for "adulting."

Bay Buchanan told me the story of how many younger employees of her brother Pat's political campaigns had high expectations for their entry-level role. Hired as an office assistant, after six weeks they were looking to be promoted and work on what they viewed as more meaningful work. However, the position the office needed was someone who could get lunch every day. Bay said that what many failed to see is how that small task contributed to the larger mission of the campaign and set them up as an integral part of it. There is huge value in becoming the person who can be depended on to get lunch on time and check the order to make sure everything is right. Eventually, when another task requires a dependable person, the lunch fetcher will be the first to come to mind.

In a modern job, one of these small tasks might be responding to a client's email swiftly. The client comes to view the employee as helpful and a positive aspect of doing business with the company, especially compared to other vendors. When it's time to continue or expand the relationship with the client, the employee will be more likely to sit in on meetings and presentations as a subtle reminder to the client that the company can be trusted to expand their relationship.

Many people view their actions as their identity. Encourage them to identify as the machine, not the cog.

Praise Finishing, Not Starting

Receiving participation trophies was in full force for younger generations. Gen Xers must be understanding because we and younger boomers started this trend. It was an overcorrection on our part. To their credit, those who received participation trophies eventually viewed them as meaningless. Similarly, misplaced and overused praise loses its meaning.

Instead, practice good, old-fashioned positive reinforcement with an emphasis on winning not playing. It may hurt their feelings at first, but it will train their brain to value finishing not participating or simply starting a project.

Throw Them in the Pool

Former Apple CEO Steve Jobs said, "The greatest people are self-managing. They don't need to be managed. Once they know what to do, they'll go figure out how to do it."

A lingering effect of their participation trophy era is fear of failure. The way you get used to something is to do it more. Rather than ask for the answer, encourage them to find it on their own.

As someone who has fallen into the work mommy role, my behavior can be the catalyst for whether they approach a problem independently or with training wheels. Kids grew up not knowing how to do laundry or drive because someone did it for them. As work mommy, I may prioritize something being finished and simply do it myself rather than explain (and re-explain) how to do it. Instead, lay the groundwork for the self-managed employee to start, fail, start, fail, start, figure it out, finish. This means giving a little more grace on deadlines and letting them fly the nest, make mistakes, and ask questions. Most importantly, it means work mommy needs to let go and throw them in the pool. In the words of Maria Montessori, "The greatest sign of success for a teacher is to be able to say, 'The children are now working as if I did not exist.'"

Don't Micromanage Their Technology

I seem to be the only one who doesn't use my screen in dark mode. I can't even imagine having more than three or four tabs open in a browser. I'm also the only one who despises organizing email by conversation rather than individually. When a coworker or employee misses something, my first reaction is to inquire about their process, compare it to mine, and suggest they try it my way. This never works. Instead, focus on the desired outcome and encourage them to use their technology, apps, and hacks to finish a project or remember to do a task. There are lots of apps to gamify work tasks. Let go of the stress caused by their process and focus on the outcome.

Give Them More Responsibility

We live in a time of a millennial vice president and a Gen Z press secretary. The key might be to give some employees more responsibility rather than less. Put them in charge of a project or cross-project task, such as designing all slide decks for presentations. This gives them the freedom to be in charge and show that you value and trust their skills. This also divorces you from the process and to be focused on the finished product. Does it really matter if they did it in dark mode while eating Takis at 9:00 p.m.?

Don't Be the Cool Work Mommy

A 2023 Resume Lab study revealed that 83 percent of Gen Z workers consider themselves job-hoppers, with 43 percent intending to stay at their current job for just two years. This aligns with a 2024 Self Financial survey, which found that while 84 percent of Gen Z expressed loyalty to their employers—only slightly lower than the 88 percent reported by older generations—their higher quitting rates suggest a growing dissatisfaction with unmet workplace expectations.

If you are the manager or boss, act that way. You are not their friend and they don't have the same allegiance to a job that past generations may have had. Not being the cool work mommy means not oversharing about life outside of work, asking them about their personal life, or using Gen Z lingo—you're probably using it wrong anyway. It also means correcting them when their behavior crosses the line of professionality.

DOES THIS EMOJI MAKE ME LOOK OLD?

In his book, *The Anxious Generation: How the Great Rewiring of Childhood Is Causing an Epidemic of Mental Illness*, Jonathan Haidt wrote, "We are physical, embodied creatures who evolved to use our hands, facial expressions, and head movements as communication channels, responding in real time to the similar movements of our partners. Gen Z is learning to pick emojis instead."

As use of emojis increase in the workplace, we're learning that younger generations have deeply held beliefs about them. I've used a "thumbs-up" as "got it" and it has been perceived as dismissive and led to hurt feelings. The Daily Mail reported, "[Sending] a thumbs-up can be seen as passive aggressive and even confrontational, according to Gen Z[,] who claim they feel attacked whenever it is used[...]."

One Reddit user wrote the thumbs up emoji is "hurtful." He added, "No one my age in the office does it, but the Gen X people always do it. Took me a bit to adjust and get [it] out of my head that it means they're mad at me."

On the receiving side, Gen X is also adapting to their communication. For example, "lol" doesn't necessarily mean "laughing out loud"—Gen Zers often use it as a period at the end of a lighthearted sentence. Gen Xers perceive it as not taking something seriously. Knowing their intention can save some frustration when receiving a text like "Finally finished that report lol."

Another instance that has frustrated me to the point of calling a team meeting (so very boomer of me) is the overuse of the phrase "my bad." Millennials and Gen Zers mean it as "I'm sorry," while Gen Xers and boomers perceive it as not understanding the gravity of a mistake and not fully taking accountability.

Always keep in mind when interacting with Gen Z and millennials that they are sensitive or anxious in new situations like the workplace, and more likely to seek alternate meanings by reading between the lines to enforce their views or anxiety about a situation. To test this, the next time an employee makes a PTO request or says they won't be able to meet a deadline, write back "K." It will totally ruin their vibe.

The slang divide today is even greater than when we first entered the workforce. I now sympathize with the boomers who expressed confusion when "bad" could also be used as "good." One advantage they had, though, is that Gen X was less likely to use it in the workplace. For all their talk on work-life balance, Gen Z and younger millennials are more likely to blur the lines between social language and business language.

Here are some examples of slang* I've encountered in the workplace:

Bet
Definition: *Okay, cool, I'm on board*
Example:
"Can you get this done before the end of the day?"
"Bet."

Gucci
Definition: *Good, all is well*
Example:
"Do we have everything we need for this meeting?"
"We're Gucci."

Yeet
Definition: *To express energy or enthusiasm, but can also be used sarcastically*
Example:
"Can you meet with the client next week?"
"Yeet, let's do it."

Periodt
Definition: *To express a mic drop moment, finality, or end of discussion in a positive way*

Example:

"Which version of the logo do you think we should use?

"The black and white one, periodt."

Bussin

Definition: *Really good, amazing, previously known as "fire"*

Example:

"How did Madison do on the presentation?"

"Deck was bussin. She killed it."

Sus

Definition: *Suspicious or suspect*

Example:

"These sales figures seem off."

"Yeah, total is definitely sus."

No cap

Definition: *For real, honestly, a truth bomb*

Example:

"Do you think we'll hit our sales goal this quarter?"

"It'll be tough, no cap, but I'm trying to get that bonus."

Rizz

Definition: *Charm, charismatic*

Example:

"How were you able to get that client on board so quickly?"

"I just him them with the rizz."

Finna
Definition: *Planning to, fixing to, about to do something*
Example:
"What are you doing this morning?"
"Finna smash this report before lunch, yeet."

Drip
Definition: *Style, swagger*
Example:
"How is the campaign looking?"
"Branding's got drip, periodt."

*These may have changed meaning, usage, and popularity by the time of printing.

As Gen Xers, we're more likely than boomers to seek out the meaning of these words and let go of their illogical origin. At least "bad" could be explained easily as "it means the opposite." Imagine how future generations will explain the etymology of "bussin."

Gen X managers may use Gen Z slang sarcastically, but it is now up to us to define what is appropriate in the workplace. Don't be cool work mommy and try to use these words. Set a standard for workplace communication and they'll follow. Show them your leadership vibes, rizz, and that you won't hesitate to fire someone who doesn't work to your standards. Periodt.

THE GREAT BOOMER WEALTH TRANSFER: DON'T COUNT ON IT

As baby boomers age, some experts are warning that Gen X isn't prepared for the "Great Wealth Transfer." In a 2023 article from Kiplinger, a financial planner discussed the importance of generational wealth transfer planning for Gen X in light of wealth transferring from boomers to younger generations. The author argues that the transfer of around $84 trillion will significantly impact the financial landscape. Mark Kenney wrote, "As recipients of this wealth transfer, we will be in a position to manage and invest significant sums of money. However, it's money many of my fellow Gen Xers will probably be new to managing. This means there will likely be a plethora of challenges to maintaining the newly transferred wealth."

Baby boomers letting go of their amassed fortunes? As Carl the janitor said, "Don't count on it."

According to the Federal Reserve in late 2024, baby boomers controlled 51 percent of US wealth ($82 trillion). However, AARP found that baby boomers using LendingTree saw debt rise $8,848 (nearly 7 percent) during the pandemic, driven by mortgages (over 70 percent of total debt), unlike Gen Z, millennials, and Gen X, who reduced borrowing. Investopedia also noted that much of the boomers' fortunes is held by the ultrawealthy.

Unlike younger generations, many boomers own homes outright. However, even in economic downturns, boomers choose to maintain or increase their lifestyle spending. And why not? They deserve it after decades in the workforce, as any of them will tell you! Some experts speculate that when mortgage rates dipped down, many boomers upgraded their living situation, contributing to their mortgage debt going up. Experian data also showed their personal loan debt is 18 percent higher than the national average.

Investopedia reported, "The [b]aby [b]oomer generation may have been the biggest beneficiary of four decades of wealth transfer, and as a result, their spending is rising while other groups are consuming less, according to analysts from Bank of America."

Baby boomers hit the jackpot, snagging $8 to 10 trillion from their Greatest Generation and Silent Generation parents. Meanwhile, Gen X and millennials may await an estimated $84 trillion fortune on paper, but boomers aren't slowing down their spending in retirement. Boomers got a hefty slice of a smaller pie, debt-free, while their kids will inherit (if it's still there) a much smaller piece of a larger pie—less dough per person.

Since many boomers are retired, they spend significantly on travel, contributing $120 billion annually to leisure tourism, and favor dining out and on premises alcohol consumption. Wealthier boomers splurge more, but median savings hover at $194,000, per 2024 TransAmerica data. Social Security also remains a crucial part of their income. Their spending balances frugality and enjoyment, reflecting both their financial security and concerns about outliving their savings. Bankrate's 2024 Annual Emergency Savings Report showed that 37 percent regret not saving more.

But it's not necessarily because they wish they had more to give. Barron's reported, "Giving money to the next generation while still alive is a more common move for young people now than it was for older generations. Wealthy people ages [twenty-seven] to [fifty-eight] are more than twice as likely to say they want to share their wealth with the next generation during their lives compared with people ages [fifty-nine] to [seventy-six], according to a recent survey from Charles Schwab of people with at least $1 million. Those wealthy older people are more likely to say they want to enjoy their money themselves during their lifetime."

Latchkey kids will be latchkey retirees and, possibly, helicopter investors for our children. We can also flip the script on the retirement savings course laid out for us. Many boomers got the security of the same job all of their working life, complete with a 401(k) match; we didn't. However, we do get to have lots of revenue streams and not be bound by one job, one income, and one way to work and retire.

CHOOSE YOUR OWN RETIREMENT ADVENTURE

Gen Xers are now being wooed by retirement communities. Pew Research Center projects Gen X will outnumber baby boomers by 2028—63.9 million of us to their 62.9 million. *MarketWatch* reported that builders are scrambling to ditch the boomer bingo nights for something more our speed—pickleball courts, firepits, and "pocket offices" for those still working.

Among the aesthetic changes are getting rid of dining rooms in favor of dog washing stations with a mid-century modern vibe. They are also including more physically-demanding workout areas, like walking and hiking trails and fitness bars.

However, not everyone may be able to afford to live in the Gen X villages. A British survey estimated that only 28 percent of Gen Xers are on pace to reach retirement savings goals. A third are clueless about what they'll need, 17 percent think they'll work forever, and 25 percent have no estimate of when they'll retire.

You may still be a few years out, but perhaps you're curious about your retirement future. YOU are in charge of how your retirement adventure will play out and end. At any time, you can go back and make a different decision to see what other retirement paths await you.

Turn the page and let the adventure begin!

You are at the beginning of your Golden Age. You just finished reading an amazing book and bought ten more copies to lovingly distribute to friends. You're motivated to begin a journey of human fulfillment and lay the groundwork for your best life. You pause because you feel a pinch in your neck and wonder what you did. Did you sleep on it wrong? You remember it happened when you reached for the towel in same way you always do while getting out of the shower.

You begin dreaming about the next ten to fifteen years as you prepare for retirement. You know you want to maintain your lifestyle, maybe even indulge in a few luxuries. Are you financially prepared to live another thirty years?

If yes, go to page A.

If no, go to page B.

Page A

Congratulations! You are in a fantastic position to begin your retirement adventure. You glance at the clock. It's nearly 8:00 a.m. and Aiden and Olivia still have not come downstairs. You call out that they'll be late for school.

Aiden comes down first. He's wearing Crocs and a shirt that says "Ally." Olivia is next, large headphones already on her faded pink hair.

"What do you want for breakfast?" you ask.

They mumble and head to the car.

As the three of you sit in the school pick up line, you ask Olivia how college applications are going.

She rolls her eyes and says, "I need a break from all the pressure. Me and Chloe are going to take a gap year or two. I don't know." She opens the door to get out and says, "Also, can you start dropping me and Aiden off separately?"

"Why?" you ask.

"He's creeping out my friends with all his talk about being a male feminist. It's weird, especially for a senior."

Aiden says nothing as he swipes to the right over and over on his phone.

You realize that you may not be as financially prepared as you thought as you calculate the prospect of your daughter living at home at least another two years and having no means of transportation without a driver's license. You also wonder what kind of legal bills Aiden's commitment as a male feminist might accrue.

As you pull out of the school pickup line, you contemplate your next move. The phone rings. It's the president.

"I need you on my team," he says.

Working for the administration? As a Gen Xer, do you really want to be part of the system you told yourself you'd fight?

If yes, go to page C.

If no, go to page D.

Page B

Yikes. You realize you spent too many years in your dream job, sometimes scrimping, but not really saving. You're in a comfortable job now, but maybe you should start a side hustle to squirrel away some additional income for the future. You picture you and the love of your life on the porch of a beachfront home, several rescue dogs underfoot. The ping of your phone knocks you out of your fantasy.

"Should I answer the client or wait until you get here?" Saffron asks.

You sigh. "You can answer," you write.

"K. What should I say?"

You put down the phone and ask Grok, "What are some creative side hustles that don't crush my soul?"

Grok replies:

Custom Art or Illustration
Handmade Crafts or Jewelry
Creating Digital Products (Printables, Stickers, or Templates)
Teaching an Online Course

You really aren't good with drawing or crafts. You like the idea of digital products or teaching a skill because it doesn't involve any upfront costs.

If you decide to create a digital product, turn to page E.
If you decide to teach an online course, turn to page F.

Page C

"What is the salary and the benefits?" you ask the president.

"Look, my Cabinet members, the best people, tremendous people, they're making $246,400 a year—big money, more than those senators and congresspeople stuck at $174,000, okay?"

"Yeah, that's great," you tell him. "I just worry about being a Gen Xer in that bureaucracy."

"We're fixing it. I pick Gen X winners like Sean Duffy for secretary of transportation—fantastic guy—and Tulsi Gabbard for director of national intelligence—amazing, strong leader. Gen Xers love me. Just ask Melania! Remember when I got Pete Hegseth for secretary of defense? People said I couldn't get him. I got him. I only pick the best. Plus, they get incredible benefits—loan forgiveness, holidays, parental leave—great stuff. Tremendous!"

"I'm inclined to say yes," you tell him. His unshakeable confidence is infectious.

"You'd be crazy not to take it," he tells you.

"Okay, I'll do it. Do I have to move to DC though?"

"DC? Overrated. Swampy mess, terrible traffic—honestly, you're smart not to want to move there. But this job? You don't need to be there to win big."

"So, you and the vice president are okay with me taking a job as commissioner of the Social Security Administration with the intention of destroying it? Giving people the power to invest all of their money?"

The President is silent. Then he says, "Destroy the SSA? Bold, very bold—I like it. Big government, total disaster, bleeding money out of everywhere. You want to take it down? Go in there, wreck it, make 'em cry."

And that's what you do. You become a hero to Gen X and all future generations. Galveston County, Texas, the only county that allowed federal employees to opt out of paying Social Security taxes in 1981, renames a county building and park after you. The grand San Luis Spa and Resort gives you an ocean view suite for life, complete with complimentary spa services and room service until you die.

The End

Page D

You're flattered that the President would think of you but you can't imagine what Aiden and Olivia would think. You scold yourself for caring—you used to be a rebel. Before the school pick up line, you were passing everyone standing in line at any function—a restaurant, a club, a concert (you didn't even go in through the front!). You were part of the *it* crowd. Now you're reminding virgins who can't drive to eat their breakfast. You look at your loyal chocolate Lab, Buster, in the backseat. He still appreciates you.

When you and Buster get home, the Gen Z energy of the house merges with your Gen X soul. You open Instagram and post a live video about your feelings about kids these days. You put the phone down and feel relief. If anything, the twenty-five people who follow you will be amused.

Hours pass as you immerse yourself in work. You realize it's nearly time for lunch. You pick up your phone to check the time.

Seventy-seven text messages?

Eleven voicemails?

You unlock your phone. Apparently, your rant has gone viral. You now have over 200,000 followers. There are a flood of messages agreeing with you. A few are saying you're hurting people's feelings and that you should kill yourself.

Among the DMs is one from someone at Fox. It's a producer asking if you'll come on the late-night show to talk about going viral at fifty.

If you agree to do the show, go to page G.

If you decline the show, go to page H.

Page E

I can write a digital toolkit, you think. Every fellow Gen Xer you talk to complains about how hard it is to communicate with their employees. It's like walking on eggshells to not hurt their feelings or cross a line in the workplace. You down a Diet Coke and get to work.

By morning, you've designed spreadsheets for task management. You have a list of coupons to hand out to younger employees who crave encouragement and rewards, such as a one-hour nap break or smoothie recipe for self-care. You've written flowcharts for finding an answer independently and setting benchmarks for success, like writing an email without the net of feedback from your superior.

You post on Etsy. You're excited by the prospect of mailbox money. You've done the work once and now it will be a steady stream of income to help supplement your retirement. Maybe others will be inspired to find their own revenue stream in the digital age!

The next morning you receive an email from HR.

> *Both Saffron and Zephyr reached out to the Work Experience and Purpose Team (WEPT) regarding a "digital toolkit for cross-generational management." Saffron said they felt personally attacked and will not be signing on the rest of the week to process their feelings. Zephyr is willing to work today in exchange for a bonus wellness day during spring break. He reiterated that this is already a difficult time for him as he makes the transition to post-college work life that doesn't build spring break into their work schedules.*

As such, the company is requesting you also take time off to contemplate how our actions as mentors and team leaders can affect others.

This will not be considered paid time off.

You close your laptop and, do, indeed, contemplate how your actions led you here.

The End

Page F

You think about all the wisdom you have to offer. Can you teach a skill? You brush a crumb off your XX-XY Athletics Legit Leggings. You pat yourself on the back for already being ready for a workout despite the serious turn this day has taken. You remember Ethan Suplee's (from the *American Glutton* podcast) Prep Deck. You can teach people to be lazy! But in a good way. A way that makes their life better. You're Gen X and the slacker label has been put on you but you also have the drive to do better in your own time.

Over the course of the next few weeks, you record a series called "The Slacker's Guide to Health and Fitness." You post on a skill sharing site. It catches the eye of the producer for the number-one late night show—*Gutfeld!* They want you to be on the show.

If you agree to do the show, go to page G.

If you decline the show, go to page H.

Page G

When you enter the studio at Fox, you're first taken to the hair and makeup room. The team gives you the confidence to hang with Gen X royalty—Greg Gutfeld, Lisa Kennedy, and Rachel Campos-Duffy.

After the show, you walk back to your neighborhood. It's a clear, crisp night. The smell of garbage and marijuana fills the New York City air. You consider your new venture and what it means for your future. You've been in New York over twenty years. Your second act is just taking off and you could do it anywhere—and cheaper. A comfortable retirement in New York seems unlikely. At least in a state like Florida or Texas there's the prospect of owning a house outright one day. You're also the age when the cold is starting to get to you. You now understand what "bone-chilling cold" means.

If you stay in New York, go to page I.

If you leave New York, go to page J.

Page H

So much for being the risk taker you always prided yourself on being. Is there any more Gen X left in you? The adventure is over for you. You've settled into a life of checking your paltry mutual fund daily in the hopes that it might be on the upswing as each day ticks by. Once a criticizer of Social Security, you come to terms with it being your main income in only a few short years. Screw future generations, it's owed to you.

The End

Page I

You could never leave New York. It's the whole package. The culture's unmatched—museums like the Met, theater on Broadway that people fly across the world to see. The food's amazing—you can drop a fortune on a meal or grab a perfect bagel for pocket change at any hour. The energy's nonstop. Sure, there is insane rent, dirty snow, the occasional rat—but you take it in stride. It's just part of the magic of the city!

Every day is its own adventure—dinner might be some hidden gem in Queens or a spot in the Village you've never heard of, and then you'll casually mention it like it's no big deal. Living here's a point of Gen X pride, too—New York's the center of everything. Sure, you'll grumble about the cost or the crowds, but deep down, you wouldn't trade it. It's like living in a movie.

You see a sketchy group of young men with a bike chain and a tire iron as you cross the road. *Don't make eye contact*, you tell yourself, before all goes black.

The End

Page J

Leaving the city has been on your mind for a while. As you get older, the grittiness of the city is no longer appealing. Leaving the comfort and predictability of the city and moving to a red state is now the rebellious choice.

Texas is the obvious choice. It doesn't have a state income tax, the cost of living is cheaper, it has beaches, and it has its own culture. And if you ever miss the smells and homelessness of New York, you can visit Houston or Austin. If you miss the traffic of New York, you can visit Dallas.

Your lease is up in a few months and you start preparing for the nearly cross-country move. It's an adventure and it feels pretty good to be taking this risk when you're middle-aged. You really do feel like it's a new beginning—your second act.

You thrive in Texas. You're an hour from the city, but have all the normal day-to-day conveniences in one of hundreds of cities and towns of Texas. They all have their unique flavor and you enjoy exploring them.

Your Golden Age is just beginning and the freedom of small(ish) town life gives you the opportunity to start saving money. By the end of the year, you have enough to start an IRA. And the next year, you add to it.

Your rebellious second act is upon you. You put down this book and begin.

The End

EPILOGUE AND ACKNOWLEDGMENTS

Author and habit-building guru James Clear said, "You are as old as the risks you take. In many ways, aging is not the process of growing old, but rather the slow death of becoming overly protective, scared, and worried about losing what you have. Youth is found in the energy of going for it, taking the risk, and trusting that you'll figure it out along the way."

You don't have time to wait! Embrace middle age with optimism like Ferris Bueller, a distrust of authority like John Bender, and an entrepreneurial spirit like Joel Goodsen.

I couldn't write an epilogue without mentioning those who have helped me figure it out along the way. I wouldn't have the confidence and desire to write this book if it wasn't for Brett R. Smith—the Keith to my Watts. He is my fellow pop culture warrior and political punk. To quote Emily Brontë, "Whatever our souls are made of, his and mine are the same." I am especially thankful he brought a cattle dog named Cora into my life.

Special thanks to Brett R. Smith and Eric Weathers for collaborating on an amazing book cover. I've never looked so good! Thank you to Ivan for the illustrations throughout the book.

Thank you to those who read early drafts and gave it their endorsement—Rachel Campos-Duffy, Ethan Suplee, Robert Davi, Terry Schappert, and Jennifer Sey.

Thank you to those who have encouraged and inspired me over the years—Lisa Duncan, Greg Gutfeld, Elissa Scannell, Lisa Kennedy, Chris Barron, Shawn Gardner and their dogs, Jenna Stocker, Danielle Schubring, Ann Coulter, Thaddeus McCotter, Scott Adams, Paul Erickson, Michael Malice, Kurt Schlichter and his wonderful wife Irina, among many others.

Thank you to my publicists, Ellie Bufkin and Mitchell Jackson, for taking on the challenge.

Finally, sincere thanks to the Post Hill Press team for the freedom to write a book on the most important and ignored generation—Generation X.

You're still here?

It's over. Go home. Go.

ABOUT THE AUTHOR

Lisa De Pasquale is a writer. She has been a guest on Fox News and Fox Business, including the number-one late-night show, *Gutfeld!*.

She is the founder of BRIGHT, a daily email that focuses on culture, lifestyle, and national news. She was the director of the Conservative Political Action Conference (CPAC) from 2006 to 2011.

De Pasquale is the author of several books, including *The Social Justice Warrior Handbook*, *I Wish I Might*, and *Finding Mr. Righteous*.

In 2010, she was named a "Rising Star" by *Campaigns & Elections* magazine in their annual list of top political leaders under thirty-five. She is no longer under thirty-five.